M3: Making Marriage Meaningful

Also by Jerry Adamson, D. Min.

Adamson Family Fables
Stories to help little ones grow up right
2004

Christmas Makes the Whole World Sing
2012

Ten years writing Newspaper articles for
7 newspapers

"Biblical Ponderings"
"A Funny Thing Happened on my way to Ministry"
"Making a Marriage Meaningful"

M3: Making Marriage Meaningful

Dr. Jerry Adamson

CROSSBOOKS
PUBLISHING

CrossBooks™
A Division of LifeWay
1663 Liberty Drive
Bloomington, IN 47403
www.crossbooks.com
Phone: 1-866-879-0502

All Scripture references except when noted are taken from the Holy Bible, New American Standard Version, Copyright 1977.

In your private devotional time please feel at liberty to use the Bible translation with which you are most comfortable. Preferably use one with wide margins so you can respond in notes to what you learn and your action plan.

First published by CrossBooks 8/6/2013

ISBN: 978-1-4627-3015-5 (sc)
ISBN: 978-1-4627-3017-9 (hc)
ISBN: 978-1-4627-3016-2 (e)

Library of Congress Control Number: 2013913316

Printed in the United States of America.

This book is printed on acid-free paper.

Dedication

I wish to dedicate this book to Bro. Richard P. Oldham, a wise counselor, my friend, and the pastor who provided Judy and me with the first marital counsel we received there in his office late after several services at Glendale Baptist Church in Bowling Green, Kentucky prior to our wedding on July 17, 1970. May his counsel and the wisdom of a multitude of others who poured into my life from each classroom instructor through five different degrees, every conference speaker, and the authors of books I have read be shared now, and received with profit into your life.

My hat is also tipped to the variety of married couples I have encountered as counselees on my journey, who have helped to refine the material in this book, and which is now passed along to you with the prayer that your marriage will be filled with all that the originator of marriage intended.

A special salute to my spouse Judy, who has done more than them all to make my views on marriage realistic, as the rough edges are continuing to be whittled away from my hard exterior.

Dr. Jerry Adamson

Table of Contents

Helpful Hints for Fun in Your Marriage

Some Dysfunctions in Marriage Conjunctions

Much to do about the Kids

Taking your Marriage to a Deeper Level

Taking it through the Stages

Foreword

"Jerry Adamson is an insightful counselor, a biblical preacher and a tremendous encourager. *Making Marriage Meaningful* is the product of a man of God who loves people and celebrates marriage. This book will make a joyful difference in your home."

Pastor Hollie Miller
Sevier Heights Baptist Church
Knoxville, TN

****

"Distilling the essence of what makes—or breaks—a strong relationship, Jerry Adamson addresses the stuff of real life in *Making Marriage Meaningful*. The book breathes his contagious enthusiasm for life. His pastoral passion, biblical wisdom, and real-world savvy come through in every line. It is profoundly simple in its design and simply profound in its message. Heeding its wise counsel will strengthen your marriage!"

Sing
Roger S. ("Sing") Oldham
Vice President for Convention Communications and Relations
Executive Committee of the Southern Baptist Convention

****

"The book is excellent!"

Dr. Kevin W Cosby
Senior Pastor, St. Stephen Church and
President of Simmons College, Louisville KY

Preface

*"These pages are snapshot devotions made
up from short articles, which first appeared in
weekly newspapers and expanded herein."*

*I have to admit that there are two reasons for this book. First, God began to lay
on my heart during a variety of counseling sessions the need I was seeing in 21st
century couples for a simple and practical guide to pull off a successful marriage. It
appeared that a basic discussion of the ingredients which are necessary to make a
marriage work could be placed in a short readable book to widen the opportunity
to help all marriages thrive.*

*There are very few marriages that could not flourish if only the couple would
devote time, and energy into making it what God intended it to be for both parts
of the couple. Whether this is your first or your fifteenth marriage the principles
included provide a basic dictionary for marriages.*

*A second reason for this work is so my grandchildren (Tyler, Rylee, Haylee,
Morgan, and Ella) will know some practical lessons for their future marriage,
written by their 'Crazy Papaw'.*

M3 blends together real life practical examples of counseling issues which
either make or break a marriage relationship with a touch of humor that
makes this an easy and fun read. Dr. Adamson has spent 46 years in
ministry. The last eight years as a pastoral counselor assisting physicians,
and pastors in their helping responsibilities with hurting people.

"Now go to work on your marriage, and make it work!"

Dr. Jerry Adamson

**"Nothing in this book should be taken as a
substitute for a face to face in-office counseling
session with a caring professional."**

Introduction

This book is titled, "M to the third power—Making Marriage Meaningful." For a marriage to continue to be meaningful, grow in depth for both parties, and be productive for society it requires positive input from at least three sources: the man, the woman, and God. It is my prayer that in each page you study you may receive some small bit of instruction which will help your marriage be personally meaningful.

This booklet is blended together with real life applications, and practical examples of current issues which will either make or break a marriage relationship. Each page will proceed with a touch of humor, and provides real life answers that I hope make this an enjoyable practical read.

The following articles are bite size portions designed for couples to read privately, consider realistically, and then discuss openly over the next weeks. Each section can be seen as a simplified and constructive illumination of problems and difficulties which are seen regularly in marriage therapy sessions. Of course none of them are designed to replace the competence of a trained professional who can probe each area specifically.

Please do not assume that because I am writing on this topic, that I have never made a mistake in my marriage, or have mastered all the skill levels written herein. I am just a fellow struggler, and through the many mistakes and failures I have encountered is the reason I have learned many of these following principles. Reading material, attending classes, and listening to the discoveries of many couples has aided me in the material which is to follow.

In the past four decades, I have sought to help couples make their marriages a success. During these times I have come across eleven separate areas which seem to comprise every possible challenge that a marriage might confront. They are presented in the first major section. Every marriage may discover a glitch with either the woman, or the man, or the relationship between the two of them.

There are also four possible stress areas which begin with the letter "F" and four attitudes which start with the letter "C". They are: Family, Faith, Finances, and Familiarity. These along with the attitudes which involve: Commitment, Communication, Caring, and Change have to some degree been the source of every marriage problem I have seen. In previous years as a pastor doing pre-marriage counseling sessions we always spent some time pointing out how these areas would either make or break a marriage. Whether it was to be a healthy marriage, or end in disaster, these would determine the success or failure rate of the relationship. With this thought in mind we will deal with each of these eleven areas first in the pages ahead. Then, the following six sections deal with particular areas, and are designed to walk couples through more specific and personal areas.

The title for this book will be our guide. *Meaningful* reflects the purpose of providing a valued commodity concerning *Marriage* a divine creation. But the reward does not come automatically because *Making* it successful requires work on your part.

With hope for a brighter tomorrow for all of us, and a better marriage for you I remain,

Dr. Jerry Adamson, *pastoral counselor.*

General Turning Points

Man, Relationship, and Woman

$$2 + 3 + 4 = 9$$
$$2 + 3 + 6 = ?$$

Every marriage has at least three main components: there is a man, a woman and a relationship. It has been this way since the beginning of time. Anything more or less than this arrangement is an invitation to disaster for individuals, and the community culture in which they dwell. This may be found in the first pages of the Bible, and has also been observed in all civilizations throughout history. Family units and rituals are the key to an archaeologist's discovery.

The good news is that if any one of these components shows improvement then the marriage will get better. Some people ask me if they should come in to talk to a counselor if their mate refuses to come to the session. I say come by yourself if necessary. If you receive help and grow then you have more to offer, and the marriage has to get better in the process even if your mate stays in their same sorry condition.

Men are notorious for not coming in for counseling at the first session. They often don't think anybody else needs to know about their personal lives, and their macho attitude leads them to believe they can solve everything by themselves. What men don't realize is friends of their wives already know how bad they are, and if they could have made it better on their own, then it would not still need fixing now. If either a husband or a wife thinks the marriage needs to be worked on then it *needs* to be worked on.

I frequently instruct wives who come into counseling alone to not get angry, disappointed, or nag when they return home. I suggest if they go home after a first session, and get grilled by their hubby to simply say, "I can't remember all we talked about, but I think it may help me become a better person. If you want to know what it's like, then we need to go there together for the next session." Male curiosity usually motivates them to come the next time, and then real progress begins to be made.

Look at it mathematically. If we give the man a value of two (probably more than some men deserve), the relationship a score of three, and the woman a value of four, then we get a total score of nine. It is easy to do the math. Now let us keep the man, the sorry sucker that he is with the same score of two. Let us also allow the value of the relationship to remain three. But let's give the woman two more which brings her to six. Now the equation totals to eleven simply because one part improved. Whoever has the good sense to get help when it seems beneficial should then set the example, and start the process rolling.

The good news is that if anything improves in the marriage, then the marriage will be better. The bad news is also in the equation. If one party wants out of the marriage, then there may be nothing the other party can do to keep the marriage from dissolving. Divorce is just too easy to get if one party really wants out of the contract. Do all that is within your power to improve a marriage but do not kick yourself if things happen that are completely out of your control.

Read: 2 Peter 1:2-9 and Genesis 2:24

Pray: *"God, you created humanity and you understand every phase of my marriage. Help me to do whatever I can to make it better, and then I will trust you to do the rest. So help me Lord."*

Four "Fs" and Four "Cs"

Beyond the three major areas of a marriage: one man, one woman, and their relationship there are four areas that begin with the letter "F" and four attitudes that begin with the letter "C" where problems may arise. These eight areas either make or break a marriage. Every problem I have encountered in the past forty-six years of helping marriages succeed has fallen under one of these eleven possibilities. For this reason I plan to deal with each of these topics in the following pages first. I trust they will help to make your marriage meaningful.

These brief snapshots on marriage are not a substitute for personally seeing a family or marriage counselor. Getting a competent mutual third party who can be trusted by both people is always a step in the right direction. Often things arise in a personal session that may go unseen in a time of self evaluation. Reading books on the topic, sermons from the Bible, or attending conferences are helpful as well.

When I have the opportunity to lead "marriage conferences", I often tell the group about one book I found which carries the best material, and is most promising in helping solve the problems often encountered by a majority of people. Despite having read hundreds of counseling, self help, and marriage books, and textbooks in the areas of psychology or counseling I recommend it more than any other book. I let them know they should get a copy, if they do not have one, because it is so good for relationships. I tell them, "It can be found in all Christian book stores and many secular outlets. It is called the B-I-B-L-E." People grin and lay their ink pens down. I am serious. The Bible has a wealth of material, if we would ever dust it off, read it and put into practice what it says about developing healthy marriages and lifestyles. Remember God set the system in motion with the first man and woman. Maybe it is time to reboot the system and allow the needed upgrades to take effect. Taking a look in the Bible for answers to life might provide a great discovery similar to when a copy of Scriptures was discovered in the house of God (2 Kings 22:8).

This serves as a good place to insert that not all counselors, or self-help books on marriage are beneficial. One of the saddest stories in the Bible is found in 1 Kings 13. It tells us of a young man of God, who took some bad advice from an older prophet. Instead of keeping the clear warning from God to, "stand up, speak up, then shut up, and get out of town," before him, he let the older prophet persuade him to stick around in direct disobedience to the LORD. The young man's fate was sealed by ignorance, because he listened to a lying preacher. As he left town he met a lion on his way and was killed. Beware of listening to well meaning but false counsel.

A great turning point in the nation of Israel can be found in Nehemiah chapter eight as Ezra stands before the people, and reads from the Law (Bible). The people all stood in reverence as their joy was restored. It was their strength. They had not been guilty of rejecting it so much as they had simply neglected it. We find in verse Thirteen how the heads of households came out hungering to learn more, and applied the information to their own family lives.

The four areas to examine which begin with the letter "F" are:

FAMILY, the one you come from and the one you plan to make;

FAITH, which includes your view and relationship with your God as well as future personal and family goals;

FINANCES, where we find too much or too little makes little difference in the stress to make it stretch; and

FIMILARITY, the last area which although intended to be a dreamy pleasure can become a nightmare.

Necessary attitudes to consider beginning with "C" are:

COMMITMENT, a foundation which must be protected from the starting gate to the finish line of marriage;

CARING, must be clearly sent and received by each party in a marriage in a variety of situations;

COMMUNICATION, issues on various levels can break down relationships, and if poorly done breaks up marriages, while skill in communication builds us up to a higher plane; and

CHANGE, comes for every couple and from several directions. It must be guarded to be constructive for with every significant change in life the marriage contract must be reworked.

God established the design of marriage and set the system in motion in a garden wedding at Eden. What was started back then continues today for better, and hopefully not for the worst.

Read: Psalm 23 and John 10:10

Pray: *"God, help us to spend some time making our marriage even better for both of us."*

Family

One vital area where a marriage may be strengthened or destroyed is in the area of family. That is the family you come from and the family you make. Marriage is not just two people looking goggle-eyed at each other. It is the merging together of two different family units.

What was the name of the first school you ever attended? If you say your elementary school or kindergarten or even Sunday school then you would be wrong. The first school anyone ever attends is their *family of origin* (often written as their FOO). Many people believe basic patterns of life, and personality is established by the age of five. The roles of a mother, wife, father, or husband are initially patterned after what we see in our parents. They are our first teachers for better or worse.

Do not be distraught if you come from a broken or a dysfunctional home. Zechariah spoke a message of hope to his listeners who had been in captivity seventy years because of their father's disobedience (7:5). They would be back in the Holy Land to possess it (2:12) if they would listen, and give heed to the message of the Lord by learning from their father's errors (1:4). It is possible to realize that you have had a deficient education in your early years, and then you can decide to continue your education on family matters, and learn what a healthier life style is. A married couple might choose which family to emulate in various areas of your relationship whether it is spirituality or expressions of love.

Who does the outside labor; what are the responsibilities of each parent; whose responsibility is it to set agendas or discipline the children. Does the mother or father write the checks to pay bills? It is not unusual for new couples to have stress in areas where their different families of origin played by different rules.

What happens in a new marriage when a wife, who was raised with the tradition of putting up the Christmas tree the day after Thanksgiving, and always took it down on December twenty-sixth? But she marries a man who follows the German tradition, like Martin Luther who first placed candles as lights (not recommended by firefighters today) on trees Christmas Eve, and then you get around to taking the decorations down sometime before July Fourth.

I can just visualize it. The day after Thanksgiving for their first Christmas the bride says, "Honey why don't you go get the decorations out of storage?" He says something like, "Are you crazy? Why would I want to drag all that stuff out when it is not even December yet?" This is not a problem marriage. It is simply a collision of family cultures. So when do they put up the Christmas tree? They make a new tradition for their new but different family.

What about the family you make? So how many kids do you want? How far apart? Is adoption an option? Who will do what in their development? What happens if your plans are changed by not being able to have any, or by receiving more than you planned?

I recall doing pre-marriage counseling when I was a pastor near Winchester, Kentucky. A month before this couple were to walk down the aisle to be married I asked how many kids they planned to have.

He quickly answered, "Four" because he had three brothers and he expected to carry on that tradition. She turned toward him while her jaw dropped and then she said, "I wasn't planning on having any". She had great fears concerning childbirth. I thought I would have to split their fight up in my living room where I was counseling. They were both set on what they wanted. You would think that this might have come up while they were dating, but it waited to happen when I asked a loaded question. We will say more about issues with children in a later section.

Read: Genesis 18:17-19

Pray: *"We recognize the help our parents have been to bring us to this place in our lives. Lead us forward now, so that we might become what you want our family to be."*

Finances

The stress which comes from having pressure in the area of finances has a ripple effect that seeps into every area of our marriage life. You can have too much or too little money even though most families would like to suffer by having too much rather than too little. You can always argue over how money is used despite whether it is a small or large amount. Do you buy a new dress or a new fishing reel with that extra amount that you have?

Too much money, and pride may have gotten King Ahasuerus, mentioned in chapter One of Esther, into a severe marriage problem. He thought to flaunt his wealth before his cronies, and show off his wife as a trophy woman. She did not approve and failed to show up. The last part of the first chapter reveals the threat that created for all the other husbands, who feared their wives might follow suit in a display of an early *Women's Lib* rebellion. It is almost hilarious to read the 20th and 21st verses, and see how the king's orders pleased all the guys, but probably made all the women say, "Yeah sure". We see in the first verse of the second chapter that after he sobered up, he may have really regretted his rash actions.

Jesus spoke more about wealth and possession than He did about any subject. There will never be enough money to buy your way into Heaven, but how you handle your resources on Earth is a huge reflection of where your spiritual priorities lie (Matthew 13:44 and Luke 12:33). Look at a person's calendar or checkbook, and see what they do in their spare time, and you will learn what they really think is important.

This is why the first amount of giving should be to God as recognition in your life as to Him being in first place. If Leviticus 27:30 is valid, then any person who does not tithe steals from God, and He keeps a better balance sheet than the bank or government.

In getting to the root of marital stress you must some times peel back layers of other things that cloud the real issues. There have been couples who thought they had sexual dysfunction issues only to come to the discovery that the problem initiated in the check book. If the husband is a skin flint, and refuses to give any spending money to his wife, then he should expect that she might be a little stingy with her love. A cold husband in the bedroom may be the result of his anger toward a wife who just bounced three cold checks the past week. Almost any frustration may impact the intimacy of the marriage bed but it may not have its roots there.

Some areas which I might suggest in this brief article are not a replacement for a specific counseling session with a qualified financial specialist. One early principle is to help people realize that you can never take it with you after death. One poor widow was made to promise on her husband's death bed that she would bury all his money with him. He was such a miser. She did exactly what she promised. She wrote a check, and placed it in his casket. You can invest your wealth in heavenly causes, and thereby send it ahead, but you can not take it with you (Matthew

6:19-21). Hearses do not precede armored cars. Remember money is a good employee but a really bad master. Learn to make it work for you, and do not allow it to boss you around.

All household money should be classified as such no matter who brings in the pay check. Some arrogant men think because they went out of the house to earn money, then it is theirs despite how hard the wife at home worked to provide a place for him to return. Genesis 2:24 says the two become one flesh. Each person should have some free spending money so they will not have to account for a surprise birthday card or feel like a vagrant. But, any decision which affects the household should be made by all those with a stake in the household. It generally should not be his money and her money after you are one unit. I realize marriages late in life, and when there are children from previous marriages may alter this a little, especially in the will.

Well meaning religious men have made statements like, "God will take care of my family after I die so why do I need life insurance?" A term for them is *selfish fool*. The Bible (1 Timothy 5:8) states if you do not take care of your family (before or after death) then you have denied the faith and are worse than an unbeliever. Enjoy life today but think long term.

You can even find financial wisdom in Habakkuk (2:6-9). We do not know the tune of the mocking song mentioned there. It is about individuals who steal what is not theirs to take; try to borrow them selves out of debt; take risky business ventures; or take unfair advantage of those with less power than them. But it is clear, there is a pay day some day when all the chickens come home to roost. The other old saying of, "What goes around, comes around," also comes to mind even though there are no tunes for them either.

Unrealistic, risky, and dishonest ventures sometimes place horrible burdens on family finances. Do not try to get rich quick (Proverbs 20:21), or expect money to just come to you with out effort (Proverbs 6:9-12), or use dishonest methods to increase your worth (Proverbs 6:12-15).

Read: The book of Proverbs. One chapter a day will take you just a month to read it all.

Pray: *"Dear God, all we have has come from you. Help us to use it wisely."*

Faith

A person's faith has much to do with making or breaking a marriage bond. Everybody has a faith structure. Even an atheist has a faith in their personal belief that no god exists. People will die and have died for their political convictions and their religious beliefs. In America it is recognized that marriages may have both a civil/governmental relationship as well as a spiritual/religious one. That is why pastors, priests, rabbis, presidents of Friends congregations, and other spiritual leaders are given the legal right to officiate, and sign legal documents which make marriages legal and binding. A court official, justice of the peace, captain of a ship or I think even a pilot in flight may also do the honors.

Faith issues may arise after the couple have committed themselves to each other in marriage. If a spiritual experience or a change in religious prospective happens to one of them after marriage then the couple may need to reassess the situation, and talk about their current beliefs or life activities. Faith can not be forced upon a person if it is true faith. It must come from within each individual. There are several Bible texts which relate to couples with different religious persuasions. This in no way lessens the depth of the love the couple share, but it may require allowing for more freedoms toward each other.

An interesting story is found in the book of Ruth. A woman named Naomi went to a foreign land with her husband and two sons. The boys both married woman with the different religious beliefs of that land,

and then unfortunately all three men died. Naomi decided to head back to the home where she had family still alive. One of the daughter-in-laws stayed in her own land while the other, named Ruth went with Naomi because she had placed her faith in the ways of her dead husband and mother-in-law. The rest of the book tells how Ruth gets connected to a good man, and they foster the linage of future King David.

People hold opinions about certain things, but religious convictions are so basic to whom we are that they hold us. They are not easily altered. Religion born in a foxhole or by force is often discarded in safety or after you say, "I do".

If both people in the marriage are believers in Christ, and your spouse does something bad, then you can tell Jesus on them, and let God straighten them out. In married life there will no doubt be those times when you are pushed to the edge of all your support systems. When you get to those points of desperation, it is a blessing to be able to fall on your knees *together,* and reach up for the strength which is above and beyond you. After Solomon dedicated the Temple and completed his major construction projects the LORD appeared to him and said, *"I have heard your prayer . . . If my people who are called by My name humble themselves and pray . . . and (I) will heal their land"* (2 Chronicles 7:11-14).

Falling under the area of faith is another focus. Faith involves our dreams and hopes for tomorrow, not just our views about God. Stress is created when our dreams and aspirations for the future are not coinciding. If a man has a life goal of being a foreign missionary in another country marries a wife who has her heart set on a white picket fence surrounding a half million dollar home close to her family, there is bound to be conflict in store for them. It surprises me that so little time is given over to discussing what plans you have for the future with your intended mate who will be largely affected by any of your future decisions. Learning to dream together during later courtship and engagement can be a lot of fun. They may also change however as your lives develop.

Successful goals for the future of your marriage should include both set of values and targets that each individual wanted to achieve in their life. Remember if you see a turtle on a fence post then you can know that they did not get there on their own. Be sure to know what your spouse wants out of life, and help them get it.

Read: The Book of Ruth and Acts 18:2 & 26

Pray: *"Lord, we thank you for leading us to each other and for allowing us to both be lead by your loving hand."*

Familiarity

This topic is always discussed last during pre-marriage counseling sessions. That does not mean that it is unimportant, because the truth is just the opposite. I understand different couples have different standards so this brief piece will not be exhaustive, but do not be too naïve, nor too arrogant to fail to understand its significance. A couple or one individual can place too much emphasis or too little attention to their sex life, which can damage a marriage through either neglect or over emphasis. The importance of shared sexual fulfillment is vital in a marriage although specifics do change over the years.

Within a committed relationship of marriage is where one man and one woman should discover that all their sexual needs were intended to be satisfied according to God's original plan. That has not changed despite the sexually revolution of the 1960's, nor Hollywood's soap opera take on the matter. God knows what is best for each couple as well as what is best for society as a whole, so I do not flinch from being politically incorrect if necessary.

You need to realize an important truth right up front. Men and women are different. Boy, am I glad for that. I really noticed the difference early in my teenage years. Not only are there obvious external differences, but there are many internal and emotional differences as well. Some factors may vary from couple to couple, yet there are enough standard differences that certain general conclusions can be drawn.

The doorway into a man's sexual nature is usually through his eyes. A woman is designed where sound, touch, and relationships are the normal turn-on for her. Therefore, foreplay is important for females to experience sexual climax. A man may see that as a waste of his time, and therefore selfishly steals from his wife, and does not allow her fulfillment. A man can see a pretty girl walking down the street, in a miniskirt in a tight sweater; and get an erection to be ready for sex, while not even knowing the girl's name. A woman, being different, can be devastated by a rejection after intercourse, because she felt a significant relationship bond had been established when it was only a male's selfish fling. Ignoring how each gender is wired can cause great confusion, heartache, and hatred.

Many couples think that because they are adults, have read books, or have experimented sexually that they know how to have sex. I usually tell couples that until they have been married a few years that they do not know how to have sex. Some couples who believe they are pretty fluent in the art look at me strange. I say, "Two dogs can have intercourse but to have mutually satisfying sex requires getting to know your self, and getting to understand your bed partner takes time. Even words common to our vocabulary may be offensive to our lover as well as some dress, timing, and actions. What turns one person on may be turning the other person off." Then you add to this that sex has been portrayed as a taboo topic, or embarrassment and fear of criticism in this most sensitize subject (for both men and women but for different reasons) creates a reluctance to talk about it. Do you have a problem in this area? Leave this article in plain view next to the bed or couch. Better yet blow it up larger on a copier and put it on the bathroom mirror.

Not only should a couple become comfortable in discussing sex, but they should feel free to be creative. The same person, same place, same time, and the same position may become too routine for some couples. Seeking to meet the needs of your mate is a most logical goal if you love them, and want to cooperate with God to bless them in the most private and intimate of ways. What ever is mutually satisfying to the couple is permissible with God. He designed parts of our bodies to be focal points of pleasure. Do not deny yourselves of sexual enjoyment.

Many good books have come out recently from Christian authors which graphically address this issue. Various Scriptures give guidance in this topic, so look upon them as an instruction manual.

Read: Song of Solomon (and do not try to Spiritualize it all away) and 1 Corinthians 7:3-5

Pray: *"Thank you Lord, for making humanity the way you have, and allow us both to receive each other as a gift from our Heavenly Father who really understands us."*

Commitment

A phrase which is often used in wedding ceremonies is, "I 'whoever' take thee to be my lawfully wedded 'something'". It is then followed by promises to a variety of difficulties like better or worse; richer or poorer (some of us do not realize just how poor that might be); in times of sickness and in health, until we are parted by death. That reflects a really strong promise, a promise which is unfortunately broken all too often. It might be better in the long run if couples spent more time before the wedding trying to understanding what they were promising to each other, their families, society and God. It is not a game which allows for everybody to go their own separate way at the first sign of difficulty or disagreement. Only spoiled little brats quit early, and go running home to mommy when things do not go their way.

Law books state that society has a compelling interest in seeking to keep marriages together once they have been established. The Bible also declares this even stronger. Breaking up a marriage complicates things like the destruction of any company. Distributing assets is only a small part of the disturbance and complications to life. A divorce clutters the way a culture can function. It reduces its stability.

This is especially true if there are children involved. Some comment that the children will be better off if we parents divorce, because it will damage them if they live in a house where there is not harmony. Research reveals this is a false assumption. Children who are forced to live apart from one or both of their parents increases their likelihood of drug abuse, and reduces their grade point averages more than what some may call "living in a problem household". Parents can be so selfish in the area of their own pleasures, and normally seek self justification for their actions.

Beside why should a married couple continue to suffer through a dysfunctional marriage, when they can get some help or work on the arrangement to make it better? There are always three options when you find yourself in a marriage which is no longer meeting your needs. The *Do nothing* option says continue to be miserable, change nothing, and just continue as you are until one of you has the good sense to die and put both of you out of the misery. The *Total control* option is to just get a lawyer, and get a divorce despite what damage that might do to others. A third possibility is to *Work* on the marriage. Get some help, read a book, go to a marriage conference, seek out a counselor, ask friends for advice and to pray for you, or in some way fix what does not work before you throw in the towel. *The third choice is the one I always recommend.* Continue to work on it until it works for all those involved.

When I am in a marriage counseling session with a couple I get real quiet and ask, "Is there a third party involved that is a part of the problem?" This question is asking both the man and the woman if they have broken their promise to keep all sexual and romantic interest or actions only with each other. If there is a third party, then we need to stop, and call that person on a speaker phone, and the guilty party tells the person by phone they are never going to see them again; because they are going to work on making their marriage a success. You can not drain a bathtub until you stop the water running into it.

When both deny there is any other person in their lives; I next ask if each of them believe the other person has no outside love interest. The shocked look on the faces of some spouses reflects they did not realize a major source of conflict in their marriage was distrust. Some spouses are wrong to suspect their mates, while others need to be aware that their actions or lack of activity have created doubts in the minds of their mates.

If you are considering getting married, then it is dumb to ask if you think you are ready to tie the knot. What you should ask yourselves is, "Are we ready to stay married, and do what it takes for mutual happiness?"

Read: Matthew 19:3–12

Pray: *"Help me be true to my word or not make a promise which I am unwilling to keep."*

Communication

A line from an old movie (Cool Hand Luke) states, "What we have here is a problem with communication". Communication problems are not new. It appears that better communication would have helped Adam and Eve in the Garden of Eden. Perhaps better communication could have avoided their issues and blame shifting. Honest speech is the focus of a compliment made to a particular lady, or to a church John knew (2 John 4). He makes it toward *your children* who walk in *truth*.

Learning to talk with your spouse should begin long before the marriage starts. Unfortunately, we are still trying to place our best foot forward to impress the other person, and sometimes we fail to develop the necessary level of honest communication until after we are in a marriage. Fear and lack of ability are both hindrances in good communication.

The first and major step in healthy communication is to *listen*. Listen intellectually and with understanding. Steven Covey states it in his book, "Seek to understand before you seek to be understood." This might require being quiet long enough for the other person to process the information, and speak out an answer to you.

Choose your words carefully because you may be eating them later. Certain words create images different for different genders or people with different backgrounds. There is also that problem with failing to speak the truth in love (Ephesians 4:15). Some people are good at telling you what they believe is a truth you really need to hear but they communicate it in a bitter and hurtful way. While there are others who claim they love people so much they end up hurting them, because they never tell them the truth about things. Later in that same chapter (verse 29) you find the warning to avoid unnecessary and hurtful forms of speech.

Earning the right to be heard may be the first, and hardest lesson some ministers need to learn. It is also true in a marriage. That is why listening is a first step in communication. Timing is another primary introduction standard. It might be helpful to ask, "Is this a good time for us to talk?" People hear when they are truly ready to hear and not until. Our marriage discovered it is hard to discuss serious subjects if the husband is wearing a dumb hat or a clown nose.

Communication is more than just the words we say. Non-verbal communications make up 55% of all communication. We might say we are listening, but if our arms are folded, we have a frown on our face, or we are looking at the television; it reflects to the speaker that we are really off someplace else. It appears to them that their words are not important to us. (Read Proverbs 15:30 for further clarification.)

The next 38% of communication is revealed by the volume, tone, pitch, pace, and a few other factors. Yelling, "I told you I love you didn't I", is usually not received as sincere. Monotone motivational speakers are often unemployed.

Only the last 7% of our attempts to communicate are what we actually say with words. It is said that words can mean different things to different people, and that words may carry differently charged emotional responses. Even when we get down to the actual words themselves we need to understand that there are five levels of verbal communications. Women normally talk and listen on level three while men pretty much stay on level two. It is like ships that pass in the night and never really make contact.

Since you are asking, the first level is "No" verbal communication. Grunts do not count as verbal communication to our wives. Animals may get by with that level of communication, but not husbands unless you want to eat dog food, and sleep in the garage with the cat. You men may wonder why you are being treated like a dog. It may be because that is the level you have been communicating on.

The second level which is where most of us men are stalled is we talk in "Facts". What was the score of the game? How much do you make an hour? What do you want me to do? Listen to how loud I can burp. All these fall into this category.

Ladies enjoy level three of the communication scale. They like the level of communicating "Emotions and Feelings" which reflects the value they place on relationships. Just the mention of these freaks us guys out. You go up to a man and ask him how he feels emotionally today, and you are liable to get decked. You could hear, "It is none of your business" or "What kind of guy are you, and why do you want to know?" Again those are responses which are factually based. A wife

20

asks her husband, "How was work today?" His answers will instructor her into the facts of how much money he made, or how many hours he worked. That is if he just doesn't grunt, and shrug his shoulders while asking for the menu facts for his supper.

The expression of, "Hopes and Dreams" are part of level four in communications. You notice that at each successive level there is a higher level of trust required. The higher the level of communication you reach the greater the likelihood of being damaged by sharing. Being hurt or controlled by the information you give at a higher level requires more confidence with the listener and greater risk. Disagreeing with a known fact only means you lack proper information, but laugh at someone's feelings, or step on their dreams now that you know them can be devastating. It may create total breakdowns in future conversations.

The fifth and final level of verbal communication is "No secrets, Total transparency". When I mention this at marriage conferences somebody will usually ask, "Does anybody ever get there?" It is a precarious position. The listener then has total control over our personhood. A caution is in order. Always remember what the listener will process from the confession made. I do not believe in lying, but some things do not need to be said at all. So, be careful what information you ask to receive if you can not handle it. "You can not handle the truth", is a line from another movie.

A good illustration comes to my mind from when I was a pastor. A man might come forward during an invitation to confess that he was struggling with temptations of lust. I would read First John one, verse nine to him, pray with him, and only announce to the congregation that he was making a rededication and surrendering an area of his life to Jesus. If the next man came down front to tell me he was having problems lusting *after my wife,* then I used different methods because it caused a different response in me. I felt I should have him re-baptized by me right then. And I planned to keep him under water a long time. The communication and confession meant something different to me.

It is always a pleasure to help couples communicate better with each other. Their smiles of discovery and expressions of relief, when truth comes from their mate are refreshing to all of us. You never know for sure until you ask; so get started opening the lines of communication, and you just might be glad you did.

Read: Ephesians 4:13–32 and Matthew 13:14–18

Pray: *"Lord, allow my words to always be sweet because I might need to eat them later."*

Caring

Another "C" word which is important for a marriage is 'Caring'. Young lovers will say they really care for the other person. At first, that simply means I find satisfaction having you around because of what I get from you. A successful marriage must take on a fuller meaning than this self focused level of caring.

A dictionary reveals a few helpful parts of positive caring in marriage. To care means you have a responsibility for the well being of that other person. God placed you there to meet the needs of that person. You pay close attention to that person to the point of worry over them. There are areas of paying close attention to them; liking them; even feeling responsible to protect them. Because you care you desire them, and like to be with them. It is a really wonderful thing when two people really care for each other. This takes on many forms over the process of the years you spend together.

Real caring in a meaningful marriage is declaring my choice of wanting what is best for you, even if it might not be best for me. This might mean you decide to do what is best for the other person at your own expense. Loving until it hurts means just that. True love sacrifices for the other person, and for the long term health of the relationship. The picture of Jesus giving His life for us is the best display of this true love. Our Lord chose to die for our sins rather than skip the cross, and spend eternity without us in Heaven.

Sometimes it is easier to make the larger sacrifices like giving a kidney, than it is to make the little daily sacrifices which reflect we really care for our mates. This attitude of caring may be expressed in physical, mental, emotional, social, financial, or spiritual areas. Practice the discipline of caring for your mate in a variety of areas. Gary Chapman has excellent books on the five love languages which help couples better understand how to really communicate caring.

The little phrase, *Each for the other and both for God,* carries a wonderful truth. Are all your decisions made on the basis of what you prefer, and what is best for you? If yes, then you have a deficiency in the area of proper caring for the other key person in your life. Demanding that your spouse do better in this area also shows that you have missed the point. It is what you give, and not what you get out of the relationship which should be your prime concern.

The opposite of a caring spirit might be seen in Job's wife. She is not given a name because she deserves to be forgotten quickly. After her husband experiences huge financial reversals in several areas; loses his children to tragedy; and contracts terrible physical problems, she urges Job to just, "Curse God and die". Talk about kicking a person when they are down! Satan was smart, and cruel enough to take many good things from Job, but left his wife to add salt to his wounds.

We have personal responsibility, and control over what we can do in a marriage but we do not have control over what our spouse does. We may change a relationship by working on making us a better person, but we are not responsible for what the other person does or has under their area of control. Our responsibility is to fix ourselves, and not to always be trying to straighten out our partner.

23

Peter wrote that a Christian husband should study the needs of their wife, and treat them with respect. Failure to do this meant you jeopardize the effect of your prayers. This might mean that if you do not care for your wife, then she might be praying against you. The needs of the husband are different. They may be physical or have a supportive focus to supply ego self esteem needs in his nature, where she might need caring with an emotional or romantic slant.

Read: 1 Peter 3:1-9

Pray: *"We come to your together Lord, and ask that you continue to work in our lives, until we become what our spouse needs us to be for them."*

Change

One final topic in the eleven top targets for making marriage meaningful is the topic of *Change*. It has been said that the only thing that stays the same is that nothing stays the same. It is true that all living things are in a constant state of flux. This should not surprise or scare us. It is normal. If all things stay the same then it is either really boring or it has died. A possum lying at the side of the road for a week is not resting on a vacation, so they will be ready for real work later.

There is a security when things stay the same. You do not have to make decisions, or alter what you have found to be comfortable. It is very possible that through the changes which come to our life we discover new avenues of adventure, and new situations that may have previously gone unnoticed. The discovery we need to make is that we need the Lord to constantly help us to understand, and that He is willing and able to do just that. This truth should help us not be terrified by change.

A growing problem seen in marriages is the break up of marriages after they have been married for twenty years. This surprises many and always saddens me. One problem may be that these marriages did not know how to grow and change. They do not metamorphosis to what they could become. A richer and deeper relationship, based upon other factors than the ones which originated the desire to spend life together were never discovered.

The major bonding force for marriages to people in their twenties and thirties is physical. While in the forties and fifties it may seem to be in the mental region with logical reasons. It is just smartest or financially prudent to stay together for the kids' sake or whatever reason. We see people over sixty have less physical, and intellectual reasons for staying together. They have emotional, and spiritual reasons which serve to keep them together. It is normal for healthy marriages to change over the years.

Those marriages which end after year twenty something may have been ill for some time, and now that the last kid has left they feel there is no rationale to keep them together at the empty nest time of life. They failed to keep their love alive by growing up and older together. They allowed the variety of circumstances to intervene, and choke out time to continue in developing a growing marriage. Therefore, the marriage died a slow death of suffocation or strangulation. This did not have to happen, but it has in many cases. If you find your marriage in this state, then begin to nourish it back to full health.

In order for a marriage to get to the finish line of "Until death do us part" the couple must learn to grow and change with the changes in life style situations. This again requires work and effort. Every new development and major change to the marriage means the marriage must reinvent itself within the context of the new circumstances. When children are born; when the first, and last child leaves the home; when any of the couple's parents die, remarry, move in with you, or to a nursing home; educational degrees are completed; new jobs are won or lost; financial bottom lines go drastically up or down; houses are built or destroyed; health and physical crisis arise; new spiritual experience are revealed; major disappointments are confronted; as well as any other major shift in the structure of life comes; then a new way to do marriage within the new situation must be formatted.

Read: Hebrews 13:8 and Malachi 3:6

Pray: *"You Lord, are the only one who never changes, but we are limited to a situation which is in constant change so help us always be changing for the good."*

Establishing Proper Prospective

My Reason for Marriage Counseling

I'll do whatever it takes to save a marriage, but it is not really up to me. Possibly 99% of all marriages could be saved if the two marriage partners were willing to try, and just work together for their common good. Remember, it takes real work to make a marriage work. Sometimes it is important to get a little external help in order to make a marriage better before a rescue attempt is needed in desperation. The story has been repeated all too often where a marriage ends in premature closure (also called divorce). One or both of the people will come to a marriage counselor too late or stop the marriage sessions before real progress has been made. It results in a type of too little and too late approach. Failure to follow through on promises or procedures developed during marriage therapy is another problem which torments me with counselees.

There are three things you can do in a marriage which has become less than satisfying. You can take the *do nothing approach* and continue doing the same things while you change nothing until one of you has the decency to die, and put you both out of the misery. The opposite end is to *take total control,* and just end the marriage in a divorce. A third option is what I always recommend. Take what you have, and *work on it to make it better.* Read a book; talk to each other; attend a marriage seminar; ask a person you both trust for guidance; or see a marriage counselor. Refuse to allow your marriage to deteriorate.

Being too far down the road to divorce; coming in too late; or perhaps a lawyer or judge required that they seek counseling, may start the process for reconciliation; but too often a couple no longer even have the will to fight for their marriage, because they already threw in the towel. The state has a compelling interest in keeping the couple in a marriage. Social, legal, and financial stability lean on the foundations of successful homes, especially if kids are involved. (There are two things I can tell you about most all children whose parents get a divorce. They are written in another place, and you won't like it.)

If you ever go to a marriage counselor; I want to be one of the first to congratulate you. You might ask why you should be congratulated. It is because you have the good sense to seek help, and a desire to take your marriage and make it better. This is aided by bringing in a third party who may care about the couple, but does not have a vested interest in the relationship. When spouses have problem issues each realizes the other person wants what they say, because it is best for that person. It is hard to accept advice when you think the other person has an agenda which is best for them, but not best for you.

Some times I will look toward a wife (after I tell them not to read anything into this because on a scale of one to ten my wife is a twelve) and say, "I am not planning on going home to live with you." Then turning to the man I say that I sure am not going home to live with YOU! After they both laugh, I remind them that is why counseling works. I am only there as a counselor. By being a non-vested person I can honestly point out things that should be changed by both parties without it being beneficial to me personally.

The most basic social unit God created was the family. He initiated the family before governments or the church. If marriages are strong, then there is hope for a good society and a good church. If families operate poorly, then both governments and churches are sunk. Ministers need to remember a church can always get another minister, but if their family goes downhill then chances are the church may not want them either. If a person is out of tune with their family, then they might play off key in any orchestra. Keep your marriage at the top of your priority list.

Read: Psalm 1:1; Proverbs11:14 and 15:22

Pray: *"Lord, will you help me have the good sense to get help when it will benefit our marriage."*

Unlocking the door of love with 1 Corinthians 13

To unlock the door of love at its maximum possibility it is imperative that you discover the keys in First Corinthians 13, where it is described in detail by the author of love, God. It is there we find love is not what you get but what you give. This chapter entitled, "The Great Love Chapter" has often been read at wedding ceremonies. It tells us what love is and what love is not. If you dare to examine your love level then read on.

One of the attributes of God is that He is Love (1 John 4:8). Galatians 5:22 states an outgrowth fruit of the Holy Spirit living in the life of a believer is *love*, and then that is followed by eight other attributes which should flow from it in the life of a follower of Christ. Jesus summed up the badge of discipleship when He stated that other people will know that you belong to Him if you love each other (John 11:35). The Bible also explains that love casts out fear, and will hide a multitude of sins.

The chapter reveals the priority of love in the first three verses of 1 Corinthians 13. Despite what we say, if love is not in the forefront, then we are just a big noise of hypocrisy. In the areas of wisdom and knowledge one can look far into the future; understand past mysteries; or be a wealth of present information, yet if there is no love added, then we really know nothing of value. Should we sacrifice ourselves for others or gain vast acclaim where everybody knows our name, and still do not do it from a motivation of love, then it gets us nowhere for we still accomplish nothing.

The personality of what love is, and what it is not fills the next four verses. Effective love is patient, forgiving, and kind. Explaining what it is not forces us to look at what may drive us instead of being moved by real love. To want someone because it will make us feel good about ourselves is not love. Real love does not desire its object because of how others will then say we are so important. It does not act in a showy manner, nor act foolishly out of place to the point of embarrassing others. If you love, then you are not in the relationship for your own pleasure alone. A short fuse which causes us to explode in anger; if we do not get our way shows we did not love in the first place.

We do not keep a record of disappointments and wrongs committed against us when we really love somebody. Love does not sit around suspicious thinking bad about others out of mistrust, nor happy when we are disappointed by another's mistakes, or rejoice when we catch them messing up in order for us to prove them wrong. Love causes us to be happy and not judgmental when the other person reveals their true nature. Love protects, and trusts the other person to change for the good. If you are asking yourself, "Is this true love that I have?" then check this list out. Love is a choice, not a mere feeling of temporary infatuation.

Persistence of love is shown in verses eight through twelve. If you love Bobby this week and Jimmy next week only to fall out of love with both of them when you see Tommy; then you did not really love any of them. If it is love then it lasts through thick and thin. It does not let go, fade out or diminish. It puts up with all kinds of things; continues to believe by faith what it is told; stays around for the future with hope; and continues to endure the disappointment which will come when our lover needs our endurance and forgiveness.

Our love chapter then crescendos when it reminds us of the performance of love. Faith, hope and love are at the top of the list of godly virtues. Without faith it is impossible to please God. Hope is like an anchor that ties us to the secret mysteries of the future. But mighty love rates the highest above them all. It is the greatest. So, how does your love life stack up to this description of what true love is?

Read: 1 Corinthians 13 and reread it again

Pray: *"We both want this level of love to be truly said about the way we relate to each other."*

Work @ it, the key to success

What is in the well will eventually be drawn up in the bucket. This practical reminder instructs each individual in the marriage to invest in their own future by putting things in the well of their marriage, which they may hope to pull out at a later date. Taking the time and providing the energy to give and invest in meeting the needs of your spouse will pay off back to you at a later time.

It has been said that we will reap what we sow. We will reap only after we sow. We should reap more than we sow, and we will always reap later than we sow. If you desire a better marriage relationship, then it will require expending energy in order to accomplish that worthy goal.

To make a marriage work you must work at the marriage. Of course it is better if both parties work on the marriage. I am told that two mules properly harnessed together can pull more than the total amount which the two could pull individually. Despite whether your marriage partner is willing to pull their fair share or work on making the marriage better at all, you should work to make it better. It can not hurt the marriage, and you will definitely benefit by creating a better you. It may also allow God to use your effort to convict, and encourage your spouse to get started in working like you have shown you have been willing to do.

Lazy people expect others to do their work for them, but a marriage, like the human body, can not grow unless it has proper nutrition and exercise. A good marriage is not normally accomplished by lazy people. Paul's Second letter to the church in Thessalonica (3:10-13) had harsh words for those who were too lazy to work. His advice was that they should not be allowed to eat. Now that will change your work ethic. He also adds the encouragement to hang in there and not get weary in doing good. Nobody could word it any better as you apply it to marriage.

To expect different results when you continue to do the same old things is a mark of stupidity. If you always do what you have always done, then you will always get what you have already got. Read a book; go to a marriage conference; ask more experienced couples who you respect to mentor you; look up Bible verses on marriage; pray; or seek out a counselor who can point out areas you need to change, and assist in your progress.

Working on a marriage can be fun, exciting, and add spark to the relationship. All living things grow and change. It is much better to be green and growing than ripe and beginning to grow rotten.

You should be congratulated if you read these pages. They are not a magic wand, but they can be a start to developing a healthier home. Just as physical work will cause you to sweat, and invest time into reaching a future goal; so working on the marriage will need to include time and energy, hopefully with great success.

Read: Proverbs 6:6; 30:25 and 2 Corinthians 9:6

Pray: *"God, I don't expect to get something for nothing from my marriage, so help me work to make it better."*

Two Major Mistakes we think makes for a good Marriage

People sometimes have mistaken ideas about what creates a good marriage. They have been spoken by so many people that they are accepted without realizing just how wrong they are, and how frustrated couples become when they do not measure up to those false standards. Perhaps it will lift the load if we realize we have not violated some unrealistic rulebook.

The first mistake I hear about good marriages is that the two people are so much alike. We may start to look like each other after a few years, because we share similar finances and social levels, but we do not have to squelch each other's individuality. Try freeing your mate to be who they are, and do not buy into the mistake that you must agree on every little detail in life. Give it a rest and each other a break.

Being alike in every area does not make for a good marriage. That makes for a boring life. Knocking the rough edges off each other when there are unhealthy rough edges which need to be chipped away is typical in most healthy couples. The person who believes they are perfect, and do not need to change any thing in their personhood has been living in a self delusional fantasy world, or alone on a deserted island. Most of us need a helpmate to point out our flaws; spinach in our teeth, unwanted nose hairs, and annoying habits, which we believe we really do not have. What better person than a spouse who we love and trust to make us aware of such things.

Please do not think I am suggestion you go out, and marry the person who is the most different from you, or one who is hypercritical. The reality is that we are often attracted to those (even on a subconscious level) who complete us. It is mysterious and alluring to be with a person who we do not totally understand, although it drives us crazy at times. If you learn to blend your personal strengths and weaknesses together it can make for a mighty force in the Universe. Spending life together with someone who whistles harmony to your melody can be fun and exciting. Another individual can compliment your uniqueness as you can return the favor by helping them see the other side of some coins in life.

The other mistake some people make is thinking being in a good relationship happens when they never fight. They believe the absences of any conflict makes for a good marriage. Perhaps you have not been dating together long enough to have discovered a point where you differ. It is not uncommon to place our best foot forward, and allow little things to slide without making a fuss over the small stuff. When we date we may think love is blind, but after marriage we buy glasses. Then we see accurately that every person has a darker side of difference. Most men shave and put on clean clothes before a date, while women often use make up. Nobody looks like that when they get up in the morning.

If you have never had a discouraging word yet keep going together and some point of contention should come up, unless one of you is afraid to allow your real opinions to be expressed. One couple told me that they never fight, but you can hear their discussions a block away. As a pastor, when couples came to me before their wedding, and said we have never had a disagreement, then I made it my personal responsibility to cause them to get into a fight. If you do not know how the other person responds to disagreements, or their conflict resolution skills and habits, then you are not ready to marry them.

One major early warning signs that a couple will make it *until death due them to part* is their ability to work constructively and healthily through resolving conflict. If you fight, as all couples will, then you need to learn how to fight fair. Some examples of not fighting fair are dealt with in a later section.

Read: Exodus 17

Pray: *"Let us celebrate our differences, and merge together to cancel out the flaws which we each admit we have."*

Two Disastrous false assumptions about successful Marriages

A little unheard alarm goes off in my head when I hear words like, "I found the right person and they are perfect. Well they are perfect except for these two little areas, but I will change them after we get married. After all they made a promise they would change if we get married."

"*BUZZ*", wrong answer! That is the first major error in many marriages. We do not have the ability or the right to try and change a person. We might be able to pray, and God can change a person, but it is not our right to do so. Who are we to try, and play God by changing the person from how God made them into what we believe we want them to be?

We must take the person as they are. If they are not comfortably changed before you are married, then they most certainly are not going to change after the wedding; just because you want them to change, or they promised you they would. We used to call this evangelistic dating. Despite the real intention on the object of your affections being spiritually headed in the opposite direction you date them, believing your spiritual influence will change them. The Bible places a caution sign stating not to be unequally yoked with unbelievers. It is a reference to unbelieving members in church membership, but it can be applied as well to the area of dating. It is easier to be pulled down, than it is to be lifted up. Amos (3:3) warns that two can not walk together when they are not in agreement.

Another major error based upon a faulty assumption which people make as they contemplate marriage is they believe the person they plan to marry will make them happy and meet all their needs. If you are not a happy person, then chances are no other person in the World will make you happy. Your happiness is not the sole responsibility of your mate. That does not mean chose a person to marry that you feel will make you miserable. You should discover while dating or in an engagement period that you both derive pleasure from being together, doing things together, and enjoy common interests with similar beliefs and goals.

God does not create us to do His job as the all sufficient provider. Only the Lord has the power to meet all the needs of a person. A spouse is a vital part of that, and should be the major part, but to set a person's total value as a human is *just to exist for your selfish desires* is very self-centered. That sounds like you are either buying a slave or making a god image out of your lover. This would either violate the first of the Ten Commandments by placing your lover in the place of God himself, or the second Commandment to not make a graven image.

Of course our spouse has the function of meeting all our sexual and romantic needs, but placing all the responsibility for your life's total happiness and success on them is too demanding. Men often bond with other men as women bond with other women in social ways which are difficult to achieve by the opposite gender. A person may have friends of the opposite sex outside of the marriage, and it is not wrong or dangerous. Be cautious however not to allow any friend to subvert that closest human relationship which belongs to your spouse. Husbands and wives should be good friends, but it is not necessary for them to be your only friend. The Lord changes people. It is not our job to become a creator. God alone can meet all our needs, while other people are only His method to accomplish His will.

Read: Deuteronomy 5:1-10 and 3 John 2

Pray: *"Heavenly Father, you alone are God, and you have created both of us like you wanted us to be; so help us accept each other in that way, and trust you alone to make us what we should be."*

Three areas of the triangle of every person

It is a prayer prayed by the Apostle Paul which I pray for people, and wish they would pray it for me. It is found in 1 Thessalonians 5:23. *"Now I pray may God himself, the God of peace sanctify you through and through. May your whole spirit, soul and body be kept blameless until the coming of our Lord Jesus Christ."*

Our God understands how He made us, and is able to complete us to become everything He intended for us to become. He will set us apart *(sanctify us)* in our total being which includes our body, soul, and spirit. I am afraid this has not been taught clearly in modern Christianity, or the World. Yet it is vital in understanding who we are and how we function. John (3 John 2) prays for the prosperity of both the physical body as well as the spiritual part of his friend Gaius.

We do not have a body, soul, and spirit; we are a body, soul, and spirit. Issues may arise in any of the three areas. When someone steps on your toe it hurts your body. You can be hurt in your soul without a person ever touching you. The soul is the part of us containing our mind and emotions. We may suffer from stinking thinking or damaged emotions. *Sticks and stones may break our bones, but words may break our hearts.* The Scriptures inform us that we are created in the image of God. This is the spirit within humanity which separates us from the animal kingdom. We have the capacity of rational decision making not just instincts like animals. Humans are uniquely created. They have an opposable thumb, articulate speech, rational decision making capacity, and will live somewhere in eternity.

There are some qualities I share with a rock in the mineral kingdom. We both have weight and take up space. People grow by taking in and giving off substances just like plants. Humans share traits with the animal kingdom like mobility and mental functions. Still humans are the special creation of God in a kingdom all their own. Your dog may look like they are praying but they are not. Dogs have temperament like humans but if you use articulate speech to calmly say the house is on fire, then your dog will just rag his tail. This article may end up on the bottom of your bird cage, but it is doubtful they will become a better birdie from reading what I have written.

Discussing situations with counseling clients we try to discover root problems. A problem can be noticed in one area, but be caused by something in another part of the triangle. Stay up all night studying and you might not be able to think clearly when you take the test the next morning, because your physical body can affect your mental soul. People may suffer from psychosomatic disorders. Worry and other emotions or mental thoughts may cause a physical problem in our bodies. It is said that a broken spirit will dry up the bones. If you lose hope, and give up the will to live it may hinder the proper function of the mind or body.

It would be productive to check where the problem of the person or the marriage originated. The counterproductive activities of the husband or wife may be from a past emotional experience, or a current but yet unknown physical illness. When the Lord is involved in a marriage you can depend on spiritual resources like the Bible, prayer, Christian fellowship and godly counsel. Look for answers to your issues in the Bible, and if your spouse is giving you trouble then tell Jesus on them, and ask Him to straighten them out.

Read: Genesis 1:27; 1 Thessalonians 5:23 and Hebrews 4:12

Pray: *"God, help me to give my entire being to you from my body, soul, and spirit."*

Running from a Bear into a snake pit

Many teachers and preachers have learned the hard way about getting in the middle of a fight between two people only to be hit from both sides. The Scripture warning in Proverbs 26:17 compares this to picking up a dog by its ears. You will no doubt get bit. Being quick to run toward joining evil is just as dumb, and is opposite of the path of wisdom (according to Proverbs 1:16).

We read in Proverbs 28:1, *"The wicked flees though no one pursues, but the righteous are as bold as a lion."* This is followed in verse 17 which loosely states a guilty conscious will create fear until the day you die. Fear has its own torments, and the response to run from problems is deep in our being. It does show wisdom to avoid harmful conflict whenever possible, but there are situations where running from a problem is not the answer.

Isaiah (30:17) declared to those with a guilty conscious who reject the message of the God of justice and deceive or oppress others that a thousand would flee at the threat of just one. Both Isaiah (24:18) and Jeremiah (48:44) read almost exactly alike stating Moab might escape punishment for defiling the Lord by fleeing only to fall into a pit, or if able to crawl out they will still be caught by a snare. It seems that a person just can not escape from getting what they deserve. Sometimes you just need to stand there and take your whipping.

Denial may be the first step of most grief/crisis experiences we encounter, but sticking your head in the sand, or running away from problems in marriage rarely produces the intended positive results. It is the wrong response as well as running away, or attacking our mate with a new topic during disagreements which we feel will reduce the heat on us.

There are several passages in the Bible which are intended to reveal to us the stupidity of running from problems which have been placed in our path to develop us, as we learn from them through the process of solving them. Sometimes they are placed in our path as a way of stopping us from going in the wrong direction. Would to God we would see these temptations, and trials for what they are intended to teach us, and realistically get the help we need instead of running away, and perhaps reproducing the issue in another relationship.

Jonah comes to mind here. When the Lord called him to run an errand; he hopped a ship going the other way. His pattern seems to always be to barter with God as if Jonah knew more than the great creator. Not liking the answers he received, he always tried to justify his poor actions. Sounds all too familiar to our day when we run from shadows Satan throws at us, or toward our own selfish and short-sighted goals only to find what we want, does not satisfy us. Because most of us try to pull off a Jonah imitation at some time, then we find ourselves wishing we had a second chance as well. *So where is your Nineveh?* Then it would be wisest to head in that direction, or get ready to become fish bait.

Two humorous passages in the Bible bring this to us for our understanding. The hillbilly preacher Amos (5:19) said, *"It will be as though a man fled from a lion only to meet a bear, as though he entered his house and rested his hand on the wall only to have a snake bite him."* It appears that running away from problems into the arms of another similarly hazardous situation may be a step in the wrong direction, because we might be taking our problems along for the ride. It is possible to run off a cliff running from an invisible bear that is not really there!

Some spouses mistakenly believe that all they need is a new start. Some guys want to trade their 40 year old wife in on two 20 year olds, without realizing you will strip your gears in such an attempt. It may not occur to you but if the problem is with you, then you will not escape the problem until you get your issues fixed. You might try to run from a problem only to find the truth of Ecclesiastes 10:8 and 9. *"Whoever digs a pit may fall into it; whoever breaks through a wall may be bitten by a snake. Whoever quarries stones may be injured by them; whoever splits logs may be endangered by them."*

Read: Proverbs 17:12

Pray: *"Dear Lord, grant me the courage to face life's challenges with hope, and not be guilty of running from problems just because it looks like a safe way out."*

Helpful Hints for Fun in Your Marriage

Marriage Medicine

A four letter word will get you through a lot of heartache in your marriage. It is the word, *humor*. Being able to laugh at yourself; laugh with your mate; laugh at your mate when they will not be hurt by it; and finally laugh at the insanity of life rather than cry about those silly events which although they hurt can not be realistically changed anyway.

A sense of humor should be at the top of the list for a marriage to succeed. The Bible said it quite well 3,000 years ago, *"A merry heart does good like a medicine, but a broken spirit dries up the bones"* (Proverbs 17:22). In an attempted humorous manner I came to the lunch table one afternoon, and stated to my wife who was really trying to help me eat healthy, "I could already be in Heaven if you did not make me eat all this healthy food". Without a moment's hesitation she came back with, "But Jerry I thought living with me was like Heaven on earth". That deserved a big hug and a laugh.

Endorphins are released within our body when we laugh which positively affect our brains, and help us to process emotions and information more effectively. Use your brain to its maximum and laugh. Northwestern University did some research about fifteen years ago, and concluded through their research that people who laugh a little every day have five major medical physical benefits over those who do not laugh every day. Finally, medical science has caught up with what the Bible declared all those years ago.

Geography is filled with mountains and valleys, and all of life is filled with tears, and triumphs as well as joy, and sorrows. You can both receive all the stress, garbage, or pain in yourself and allow it to add to your grief, or share it with your marriage partner, and smile together that you have each other. Sharing laughter with your spouse will subtract from the gloom. The two of you may find nothing funny about the sad circumstances that have multiplied in your dire situation, but isn't it better to have a spouse who can share the problem, so the sadness is divided, and you only need to shoulder half of it.

Give each other permission in advance to make a silly comment the next time you hit one of those potholes in the road of life. My wife and I have the ridiculous statement which we made almost every fall for several years early on in our marriage, "If we can just make it through December with all its bills then maybe we will make it". Being on this side of some very serious tragedies in our families; we drew comfort whenever we declared that our current issues are not near as bad and desperate as those times.

The old saying is true, "Laugh and the World laughs with you; cry and you cry alone." Sometimes you just have to throw a smile over the whole mess we make of our lives along with the entire list of unanswered questions that plague you and hope for tomorrow (Acts 27:29).

Read: Proverbs 17:22

Pray: *"Give me a laugh or a smile today that I can share with my sweetheart."*

A big stick or a soft answer

President Teddy Roosevelt said, "Speak softly, but carry a big stick." At that time in the nation it was a classic statement which was greatly needed. When it comes to marriage it can be either a good or a poor idea. It is important to know which tool to use when.

Our initial stance in disagreements should be low key with soft answers like the statement begins with a soft tone. None of us should argue with the wisdom of Proverbs 15:1, *"A gentle answer turns away wrath but a harsh word stirs up anger"*. Attacking anger in your mate by receiving what might seem too strong or even hatful, and returning their verbosity with charity (love) disarms even an enemy. If you charge in, and thrust back hurt for hurt and insult for insult it is possible to raise the problem to the World War Three level. Nobody wins in a global thermal nuclear conflict. Why even begin such a mutually losing battle?

Jesus suggested a novel approach. He indicated we should turn the other cheek to offenses (Luke 6:29). This may seem like a counter-productive method to solve disagreements with painful results, yet it does not escalate a conflict. Paul quotes Proverbs 25:22 when he suggested to the Roman Christians (Romans 12:20) that to befriend an enemy heaps coals of fire on their heads. Its meaning is that they will be red with embarrassment, and rendered defenseless by your sweetness. One lady got it wrong when the pastor asked if she had ever tried this approach toward her husband. She told him, "No, but during one fuss I threw a cup of hot tea on him."

A close problem to this is the matter of gossip. Gossip is a weapon of war for cowards. Whether it is from another person, or out of your own lips, gossip can fan the flames of conflict to make matters worse. If the person talked about is not there then it is called backbiting/slander (condemned in 2 Corinthians 12:20). If a statement is hurtful not helpful; condemning instead of condoning, then it is better left unsaid. The imagery in Proverbs (26:20) is not lost on any outdoorsman, *"Without wood a fire goes out; without gossip a quarrel dies down"*.

The matter of carrying a big stick is true as well. Know what is right and be willing to fight for it. But only fight if there is no other way; then do not back down from the right. *"A sly tongue brings angry looks,"* states Proverbs 25:23. Looking mean at, and in the face of wrong and evil will often shut it up. Paul said, *"Put on the full armor of God so that when the day of evil comes you can stand"* (Ephesians 6:13). Peter calls the Devil a roaring lion who wishes to devour whoever he can. Still, we are told to resist our enemy the Devil, and stand firm in our faith (1 Peter 5:8 & 9). The psalmist poses a question of invitation. *"Who will rise up for me against the wicked? Who will take a stand for me against evil doers?"* (Psalms 94:16). President Roosevelt would say, "Bully! Bully!"

Read: Proverbs 15:1; 25:23 and 26:20

Pray: *"Please help me be willing to fight for our marriage; sometimes with a soft answer."*

Everybody is beautiful in their own way

A song when I was a teenager said, "If you want to be happy for the rest of you life, then make an ugly woman your wife. So from my personal point of view, get an ugly girl to marry you". That might make a good song but I am not sure it is a wise standard for marriage. This is a warning to some of you. If you do think this then, do not go around singing it out loud, unless you like to sleep on the couch.

Some other old sayings are these. "Everybody has their own tastes said the old lady as she kissed her cow." "Beauty is only skin deep but ugly is to the bone. Beauty lasts for only a few years, but ugly holds it's own." One person's home spun philosophy said, "Kissing don't last, but cooking do." "If my nose was blowing money then I'd blow it all on you" or "You sweat less than any fat girl I've ever dated" are not good choices for compliments either. It may be true that one man's trash is another man's treasure. If you doubt this just look in your neighbor's garage. Different strokes for different folks means people vary on what is right in a marriage partner. A person does not need fifty marriage proposals only one that works for you.

Accepting what you are, and what is of value in your mate is vital. In marriage we get the whole package. The body may be the first thing we notice in a potential mate, but after they open their mouth sometimes the deal sours. Ever person has both certain strengths and particular weaknesses. We need to realize that everybody comes as a package deal. Each person has good attributes, and weak areas in themselves that may need to be worked on throughout life. What we become as a couple is what makes the difference. Lifting up your spouse by reminding them of why you are happy to be with them not only helps your marriage partner's self esteem, but it helps you as well. If you are constantly complaining or pointing out the flaws in your spouse, then you may create a self-fulfilling prophesy, and create a Frankenstein, or begin to believe your own press releases. It is possible to be a tool to lift your mate to an even higher standard of value by placing value on them, through your words of praise for who they already are.

A problem can arise which comes from within us. Always going around putting yourself down in order to get compliments is dangerous. People may start to believe your advertisements. We understand that the opposite is also bad. Always bragging on your self may reflect pride or insecurity. Yet focusing on your self so much in self-abasement putting yourself down may not be humility, but rather a different type of pride. But it is still sinful pride.

We need to remember that God made us, and He does not make junk. I love that verse in Psalms 139:14, *"I praise you because I am fearfully and wonderfully made; your works are wonderful"*. The counter balance is found in Proverbs 27:2 *"Let another praise you, and not your own mouth; someone else, and not your own lips"*.

If you allow yourself to go to pieces when you are in temporary disfavor with your spouse, and you become a doormat in order to get them to return, then they might start thinking you are not worth very much. Desperateness is not appealing. It is devaluing and demeaning.

There are times when we need to encourage our mates. Reminding them what they mean to you, and what value they have to you goes a long way in reinforcing good habits. The old country saying states that you can get more flies with honey than you can with vinegar. Although

I for one do not know why any person in their right mind would want to attract flies in the first place.

Read: Psalm 139:12-18

Pray: *"Lord, the fact that everything you make is beautiful means even me."*

Sex is not a Hex

Huge misunderstanding still lingers from myths about what puritan ethics were when it comes to sex. Believing there is something inertly evil or sinful about sex is to misrepresent the biblical view, or to reveal what is within our own depraved minds. Both inside and outside the church, people miss some basics in Biblical Sex 101. If a person takes an unbiased look at what the Scriptures tell us about sex, then they will see sex for what it was intended to be. It is basic to life; it is normal; it is necessary in order for humanity to continue; it is fulfilling; and it is fun despite how the hype from advertisements or modern culture deranges it.

Nothing can cause embarrassment, disagreement, or anger like talking about sex. Yet none of us would be here if it were not for sex. This has been true since the beginning of time, and in every generation since then. When I write about sex I am referring to sexual intercourse as intended by the creator in its normal activity within the framework of a committed marriage. All of us realize all too well the possibility of misuse, and misappropriation of sex as it has been imitated, maligned, and misappropriated by so many. Perhaps the best place to start to present the beauty of sex, and what it is suppose to accomplish is to look at who created sex. *It was God!* Genesis 1:27, *"So God created man in His own image, in the image of God He created him; male and female He created them."* This is two chapters before sin came to humanity.

To adequately understand the nature of God we can see a reflection of Him by seeing both male and female. Sex was not initially an advertisement scheme or dreamed up by Hollywood. God did it, and He knew what He was doing. That's why the Bible is the best book on sex that has ever been written.

Some others have the misconception that sex is the magic cure-all for any and all problems. We hear this when people place their hope for a successful marriage solely on the fact that they can have an exhilarating sexual experience with a person. That is not sex as God intended it. That is just intercourse. Most anybody can have intercourse. It does not take much intelligence or training. Even two dogs in the alley can have intercourse but that is not mutually satisfying sex as it was intended by its creator.

Unfortunately, some religious people are under the impression that the whole activity is demented in some way or unholy. It is just the opposite because of who started it. Reading Hebrews 13:4 is a liberating passage of Scripture for some more prudish brethren. It says, *"Marriage should be honored by all (or in all things), and the marriage bed kept pure for God will judge the adulterer and all the sexually immoral."* The term we translate *marriage bed* is from the same word we get *coitus* which is the technical term for penetration sexual intercourse. This answers many questions in this area. If an activity is mutually satisfying to the couple, then it is ok with the Lord.

Many folks try to make a sex experience more, or less than it was intended to be. There is no doubt that the sex urge is strong. It has caused many people under its influence to make some pretty dumb sexual passion decisions. If the timing is wrong, sexual activities is like lighting a stick of dynamite, and trying to snuff out the fuse before it blows up, and destroys everybody around. It may even be stronger than the death urge, because some people will risk getting killed if others find out what is going on.

Thinking if we can just have a good sex life, then all our bad marriage issues will disappear places sex as a magic spell cure all. This view is false as well. Neither is it a curse, punishment to be endured, or a bad omen. God intended it for procreation, pleasure, and to develop personal intimacy. Sexual experiences the way God intended should be enjoyed, because four verses after God placed sex in motion He saw all that He had made, and declared it was *"very good"*.

Read: Genesis 1:27, 31 and 2:25

Pray: *"Thank you Lord!"*

Opposites Attract before they Attack

When a couple came into my office for counseling before their marriage, and made a statement like we want to get married because we are so much alike; I wanted to laugh (not out loud). Billy Graham quoted his wife when he said, "If two people agree on everything then one of them is not necessary". When two people are totally alike then the relationship is boring. Do not misunderstand the rest of this section. It is important for some general matters to find mutual agreement if there is to be success in a marriage. But God is creative, and couples need each other to fill in the voids which are missing in their own personalities.

Some men admire their girl friends and state they are so much alike that she can finish my sentences for me. "When we go out to double date she can carry the conversation, and I like that, because I am not very good at small talk," he says. Five years into the marriage he gripes, "That woman never shuts up from talking!" The thing that was attractive to him before marriage was the very thing which annoys him, and he complains about after the "I do".

Notice the girl who is not very athletic who falls for the captain of the football team. The difference is so exciting, and gets her attention since she knows so little about sports, but he knows all the scores, and can talk about it forever. Later those women come to a pastor to complain that every Monday night it has to be either football or basketball or baseball. That is all the poor dumb guy can talk about. The very thing that attracts us to each other is the very thing that drives us nuts during the marriage. That diversity is what makes things interesting, but may cause problems if we are under the mistaken idea that we must always agree on every thing. Mutual acceptance is not agreement. It is possible to agree to disagree.

Like magnets, opposites attract, and can form a strong bond. It does require merging the gears of our personhood. Similar to gears on a standard transmission you must push in the clutch to place the automobile into first gear. When you do not do this you can strip the gears, and it never fails to make an embarrassing sound. Placing a car in neutral is scary, because we are then the servant of gravity. We lose control to go either forward or backward. Yet in order to work as a team we must place ourselves into neutral sometimes, and then merge as one functioning unit, while playing to each other's strengths. Where one is weak the other typically has strength; while our strengths fill in the gaps of our mate's weaknesses. This allows the sum total of the two to be greater than what they are totaled up individually. Outsiders only see the total couple's strength, and not the weaknesses of one partner.

Learning to laugh at the individual quirks of personalities, and recognizing our uniqueness is a blessing in self discovery. Enjoy the differences. The French have a saying, "Vive La Différence". I am sure glad my wife does not look like me.

Read: Galatians 3:28 and Romans 14-15:1

Pray: *"Lord, allow us to accept, and enjoy the special qualities of each person; play to our strengths; and support one another in our weaknesses."*

Connecting and Communing with God.

It always seems like wise advice to take a problem back to the original manufacture if you discover a defect. If my car no longer has the power it once had; a strange noise is noticed which it did not previously have; or a warning light comes on, then it is best to take it into a shop. I admit there is just so much about the complications, and inter-workings of an automobile that are beyond me. They might say that you have been pushing the product beyond the intended specifications, or not doing the recommended maintenance. It is possible that you even had unrealistic expectations for the vehicle. It could be it is a problem you created, or something which is normal, and not your fault at all.

Perhaps you understand the parallel as it applies to your situation. Your marriage is not just your own creation. God is the original manufacturer of marriage. What He created He intended to work properly when the original design is realized, and directions are followed. It may be that you need to get your marriage back into the shop, and allow the creator to work on it a while.

If a product is not working properly, then it is always possible that we are doing something wrong. Forgetting the intended original purpose; avoiding road hazards; routine maintenance; unexpected accidents; inexperienced drivers with poor training; or driving with impaired judgment may cause havoc, and do damage to a marriage just like it can to a car. Taking it to the manufacturer, God seems like an intelligent thing to do. Unfortunately, many couples only do that after misuse or malfunctions have made them ready for the junk yard.

The Bible serves as a good owner's manual. Yet most of us do not read the owner's manual until something appears to be going wrong. Some people can not even find their owner's manual, because it has been so long since they read it. Do not avoid calling in the experts when a problem arises. The Lord really does care about you as individuals and your marriage. There is usually an answer, if we are willing to listen. Here are some practical suggestions.

Seek to develop your own spiritual life. Haggai chided his audience with a question. He asked since they had time to build their own houses, and take care of other affairs, then why was the House of Worship not built yet? His words, *"Consider your ways"* might well be translated today as, "Think what you are doing". Their priorities were all out of line. Read the Bible for instructions on marriage, and ask the Lord in prayer to help you. These are not magic wands, but one person seeking help is always a starting place. If your tank is empty then fill it up. Consider the reason God originally created marriage units, and why He brought you two together.

As your spouse allows, blend your spiritual work together. Start to pray together about what needs to be done. If this is hard just sit in the same room together, and privately spend time praying, and communing with God by yourself. Afterward you might begin to tell your mate what you prayed or realized. Confess your sins to each other, and the Lord. Going to a Church together is beneficial. Remember when dating that having the same basis of faith is constructive.

Respecting the diversity of religious beliefs is respectful and wise. Everybody grows at different rates. A person will die for what they truly believe politically or religiously. You can not change a person's faith. Respect each other's faith even if you do not agree with it.

A good slogan might be, "Each for the other and both for God." A beneficial verse which my wife first excitedly showed to me while we were just dating, and originally was inside our wedding rings is in Psalms 34: 3. *"O magnify the Lord with me. Come let us exalt the name of the Lord together."* Perhaps she knew more at the stage than I did.

Read: Genesis 2:15-18; 3:8; Psalms 5:3; 34:3; 55:17; 119:64 and 2 Timothy 2:15

Pray: *"Lord, move our marriage to a better place by helping me get connected to you then I believe we will have a better marriage life."*

55

The importance of Forgiveness

A concept which is ancient but greatly misunderstood is *Forgiveness*. It would be hard to escape this necessary ingredient if a couple is to be successful in marriage after about the first month of marriage. Two humans living in close proximity to each other being *fallen in their sinful nature,* and therefore self focused will invariably create a climate where forgiveness is an absolute necessity.

First, two misunderstandings are important to realize. Reconciliation is not forgiveness. We can forgive a person, and still not be able to trust them immediately. A period of time may need to pass, and a person might have to reestablish a level of trust before the relationship is back to where it was. It might be that restitution is required before the parties may move forward in a healthy relationship.

Because some people say, "I will forgive you, but I am not going to forget what you did" a second mistaken idea accompanying forgiveness has cropped up. Some believe that if you truly forgive, then you must also forget the event or transgression. This is wrong as well. Forgetting the problem for humans is not called forgiveness. It is called a brain injury.

The Lord has the ability to place behind His back, and remember our sins no more. The Scripture says that He removes our sins as far away as the East is from the West. The depth of the sea is where He cast our sins. One preacher said, "And He puts up a NO FISHING sign too". Where God has the capacity to choose and forget our wrongs we humans are not equipped to do that as yet.

Then what is Biblical Forgiveness? Biblical Forgiveness is basically three things. The forgiver *chooses* to not hold a matter over our head as a means of controlling or punishing us. It is also the choice to not use the information we have to tell others as a way to make the transgressor look bad, or elicited sympathy for ourselves. The last part may be the hardest. It is the continuing effort to not dwell on the past hurt ourselves.

Forgiveness carries two elements. It is a gift we give to the forgiven. Therefore, it is not earned by what they do to pay us back for their hurting us. It is a gift we give like grace which is given freely to us. It is also *'fore' given ness*. It may be extended prior to someone asking for it or even deserving it. You can forgive a person even before they ask. God forgives us even before we accept His forgiveness, and apply it to our lives.

This expression of forgiveness is a freeing experience for the forgiver. It is no longer being carried around, and weighing us down. We not only loose the offender for their wrong, but we no longer have to drag along the grudge, which may eat away inside us like an unseen cancer. A person who offends us may have gone on with their life, or even left this life, but we must only blame ourselves if we continue to carry on shouldering the pain of not forgiving.

For a Christian forgiveness is not an option. It is commanded by the Lord Jesus. It is not something we have the power to do in our own strength, but a follower of Christ has an internal power from the Holy Spirit to accomplish this specific task of forgiving.

When we wait for an offender to come to us, and make things right, then we enslave ourselves and yield a control in our life to that other person. It is empowering to take control, and forgive a person. Our choice to forgive places us back in the driver's seat of our destiny.

Although this all may seem impossible, it is required by God as the standard for Christians. *"Jesus looked at them and said, 'With man this is impossible, but not with God; all things are possible with God'"* (Mark 10:27). God does not ask us to do something which He knows we can not do with His help. What may seem impossible for us is an expectation our creator has for us as we allow Him to forgive through us. Jesus ties our own personal forgiveness to our choosing to forgive others. Only when we come to the place where we loose others from their debt to us can we truly begin to understand, and feel forgiven by God.

Read: The Lord's Prayer in Matthew 6:9-15

Pray: *"Oh Lord, release me from the burden I carry from my unwillingness to forgive. Help me to reach the level of forgiveness to the same degree that I have received forgiveness from you."*

Forgiveness is not an option

Forgiveness is not an option. It is a requirement for a healthy marriage. I mean get real. Do you really think that withholding forgiveness from your spouse is going to help your relationship? That sounds as if you do not believe you have ever done anything which requires your spouse to forgive you. We are all sinners by nature, and living in close quarters means we will no doubt catch each other's failures, and see each other's weak moments far more likely than those outside the home see them. We may be able to hold our breath, and keep it in for a while when we are at work, school, church, or outside. But we let it all hang out when we go behind the safety of closed doors at home.

God does not request that a Christian forgive people, it is a requirement from Him. It is best to learn how to forgive, because it benefits the offender, the relationship, and the person doing the forgiving. Philemon is pointed out by the apostle Paul (Philemon 5) as displaying an attitude of love and faith. It is in this letter where Paul then asks him to forgive his runaway slave, and put it on his personal account. This is a great picture of what Jesus has done for us transgressors. We should extend the forgiveness portion of love, because we have been forgiven of so much.

Perhaps the ultimate extreme of this grace is reflected when the marriage promise to forsake all others is broken. Yes, the Bible does give permission to a person to divorce their mate if they have committed adultery. It gives you permission, but it also commands that we forgive people who have done us wrong. The option to divorce is balanced with the advice to forgive. This may not save the marriage, nor reestablish a trust level which allows the marriage to continue, but it might start the healing process.

Matthew 6:14 and 15 really creeps me out. It states, *"For if you forgive men when they sin against you, your heavenly Father will also forgive you. But if you do not forgive men their sins, your Father will not forgive your sins."* That one will keep you up at nights.

A story from the life of Jesus is placed forward for our consideration in the dynamic that the person who is forgiven the most is the one who can love the person granting them forgiveness the most (Luke 7:41-50). It would seem that the person who is most able to forgive is the most like God. Forgiveness helps both the forgiven and the forgiver. I admit that I do not deserve the forgiveness Jesus extends to me, but I love Him because He loved me first and forgave me.

If true forgiveness is extended then it should not crawl back up at a future time to get even with the individual. This might be on the warning label from Galatians 6:1 and 2. In our ministry of restoration of someone who sins, we must consider ourselves so we would not also be tempted. That temptation may be to fail to forgive or to do so in an ungentle manner. It happens way too often that when one mate fails, and then the other one believes it is their right to do the same thing in order to even up the score. This only complicates the issue, and intensifies the problems. Beware of such foolish self-justification for sin. It comes from the accuser deceiver called Satan.

Read: Luke 7:41-50

Dare to Pray: *"Forgive me Lord, to the same degree I have forgiven others."*

How to have a Perfect Marriage

A preacher seeking to explain the Scripture which says, *"All have sinned and come short of the glory of God,"* asked his audience to raise their hand if any of them knew of a perfect man. Surprisingly one man from the back roll raised his hand. When asked who he had ever heard was a perfect man he replied, "My wife's first husband". Because memory is selective I realize people may unintentionally or on purpose forget about our own flaws. Many people in church are about three pastors behind on loyalty. They may not like the pastor they have now, and talk about how great some previous pastor was. They do not remember that they tried to get him fired back when he was there because he was not as good as old pastor so and so.

If you want to have a perfect marriage, then you will have to be perfect as well. Let me tell you in advance you will fail at perfection. We all do. The Bible states all humanity sins, and comes up short when we compare ourselves to the life which Jesus, the God/Man lived. Reality says when you take two people who are different by gender, nature, and background, then place them into a confined space; plus add that they are both sinners, who primarily want what they believe is best for themselves, and expect no disturbance; then you should not be surprised to find disagreement instead of harmony. There is going to be conflict. It is natural. Trying to make a marriage work sounds more like a mistake than a method for happiness. Still, I think marriage is not a mistake, but rather a miracle of God when it is pulled off properly. Not a walk on water miracle, but an ever day miracle where the Lord helps us transform into something better than we were yesterday.

Having a perfect marriage requires getting real with your expectations and then working together to make it happen. That means accepting your spouse for who they are, a little less than perfect just like you are. We all mess up at some point. Working on making our self as perfect or complete as we can be is where we should place our energies, and not always be trying to fix our mate. First drop those unrealistic expectations if you desire a perfect marriage. Also try adding a big dose of forgiveness to your daily routine.

A word of honest balance is applicable here as it relates to those in ministry. A verse in Titus (1:6) presents elder's/spiritual leader's families as role models. Some folks in ministry need to set their family as a priority above the work of their calling, and not just give them the leftovers after the exhaustion of ministry sets in. But those under their leadership need to realize that no family has perfect people so cut your preacher some slack, and support their family. They may live in a glass house, and always be on display which is vastly different from the cave you get to live in with your family.

There can be perfection in imperfection. That means just because each person may have limitations is no reason to believe they are less than everything they were intended to be. None of us can fly in the air without a plane (except maybe in our dreams), yet that does not make us of less value than birds. It just means we are different not incomplete or imperfect. When the King James Version of the Bible requires us to be perfect (James 1:4) it means *complete*. That means to achieve what we were intended to be. That does not mean we never do anything wrong but that we live up to the potential that our Lord created us to have. A circle or geometric design is perfect when the line comes back, and meets itself where it began.

Place your attention and energy on being what you were intended to be. In your excess time assist your spouse in helping them become not what you want to make them, but what they believe they were suppose to become. Begin making the marriage healthy for both parties by making it a number one priority in your lives as part of your way of honoring God. You should focus on self improvement before trying to fix up your spouse. Be yourself. Be your best self. Live a life beyond your self by being unselfish. When it comes to your mate remember that you can lead a horse to water but you can never make them drink. You can however motivate them by placing salt in their oats where they will want to drink.

Whenever you fail or do not achieve on your schedule what you had hoped to achieve just move on don't spend a life of regret. Nobody reaches all their goals but so what. Goals still get us pointed in the right direction, and help us to move away from where we were, and bring us closer to where we wish to be.

Read: James 1:2-5

Pray: *"Lord, help me be real with my expectations for my spouse, and work primarily on myself for creating a successful marriage."*

Train or Treadmill—Life's Goals

One person was certainly pessimistic when He stated that when he saw a light at the end of the tunnel it was no doubt a train coming to run him over. That is kind of like the sign which read, "I hope my ship comes in before my pier collapses". Cooperating to help your love mate reach their personal goals should be a part of your ambitions in life. A team must always be involved with each other reaching the goals they have set for themselves individually as well as together. Walking on a treadmill means you use a lot of energy but because the ground beneath you is going in an opposite direction you will be getting off where you got on without making any progress. The difference between a train and a treadmill is that a train makes progress.

There is also the matter of planning together what will require the effort and energy of both parts of the marriage in order to accomplish them. Believing that your partner is working against your objectives can be very frustrating, and do significant damage to a marriage. The Bible says it clearest when it says, *"Can two walk together unless they agree to do so?"* (Amos 3:3). Paul warned, (1 Corinthians 6:14) *"Do not be yoked together with unbelievers."* Even though many people violate this warning, and create a difficult journey for themselves, there is still hope that adults will act mature enough to take what they have, and work to make it the best.

If you have been reading these pages, then I hope you realize that God accepts you right where you are. Matthew 11:28 are encouraging words, *"Come to me, all you who are weary and burdened and I will give you rest"*. He does not wait until you get better for Him to start the journey with you. With God it is always best to get started now, and the sooner the better. You can not start any earlier than where you are right now. Whether this is your first marriage or whether you have made many attempts at a marriage; beginning to apply healthy principles is always the right thing to do.

Begin this exercise of goal setting by taking a good inventory of where you are currently. This is important to determine your resources. If the two of you are sharing all your assets then you can eliminate duplication of resources. Why be wasteful when you can exchange things which are no longer needed by the team. Only one pitcher can throw the ball at a time, so get a catcher if you have two pitchers, and nobody to catch the ball at home plate. Let each person play to their strengths.

Charles 'Tremendous' Jones wrote in his book, *Life is Tremendous*, "Make a decision; make it yours; and then stick to it". Unless God places big road blocks in your way do not vary from the path you have chosen. Work on it until it is accomplished. It may be set upon the shelf for a period of time, but do not leave it there too long or you may forget about it.

Henry Ford said that the person who thinks he will succeed and the person who thinks he will not succeed are both right. After all if you are not aiming at anything, then it does not really matter where you end up. We should share our short term, and our long term goals with the people who we trust, who are closest to us, and who can help us the most at arriving at those goals.

Do be realistic about your target goals. That is why the all wise God brings two different people together. We can compliment each other, and also protect each other from doing something dumb. Most all couples have a pitcher of unused items, and a collector among them to compliment each other. There is also a kite and a string in most marriages. Without the kite the string would lay on the ground, but without the string the kite will fly into a tree.

It is important to have dreams or life becomes a treadmill where we feel like a hamster in a cage wheel constantly running, but going nowhere. Realistic and obtainable dreams are important to have. They make life exciting while pulling us toward them. They do need to be realistic. Remember the old saying, "Two can only live as cheap as one if one does not eat and the other goes around naked".

Read: Matthew 11:28 and 29

Pray: *"God, allow my efforts to always be pointed in the direction you choose."*

Some Dysfunctions in Marriage Conjunctions

IN

"and, but, for, nor, or, so, yet"

Thou Shalt not Hit

If I could add a commandment to the Ten Commandments applied particularly for marriages then I might add, "Thou shalt not hit". This applies mostly toward men, because they are normally larger in frame and more aggressive. They also are more stupid than women if they believe getting physical, and intimidating your wife is a big turn on.

Any truth taken to the extreme usually ends up as an error. Being protective and providing guidance in a home by the husband who should give scriptural leadership is normally appreciated. Being abusive or making ANY forceful contact with your spouse is a crime, and should be punished by the law without feelings of guilt. Men who hurt their wives should be locked up. *Do you get the message?*

Some well meaning men misuse their authority in the household, and try to justify their sin by declaring the wife is instructed to be submissive to her husband. I agree with what the Bible says but *submission* is the willful decision of the wife to submit, and can never be demanded by a husband. If a husband demands their wife submit he has placed her in subjection. That is not submission it is slavery. Placing a person into slavery is not right. Slavery was outlawed years ago.

A wife is not to become a door mat. A husband who obeys Ephesians Five will take seriously his responsibility to love their wife like Christ loves the Church. Consider this: Christ lived His entire life in order to reflect his love to humanity. Then He died on the cross to pay for our sins. Therefore, we can not treat our wives like property or a doormat, then say we love our wives like Jesus loves us.

Proverbs 25:28 says, *"Like a city whose walls are broken down is a man who lacks self-control."* This passage may be applied in several situations. Allow me to bring it in focus here. If you hit your marriage partner, then there is no excuse for your stupidity, while the whole world sees how really dumb you are. Proverbs 16:32 warns us that controlling your temper with patience is more important than the ability to do great things like capture a city.

One should think before they strike another person. Using your fists means that you lost the verbal argument, and do not have the intelligence to admit it. One sign of the last days (2 Timothy 3:3) is that, *people will be proud, abusive . . . without self-control, brutal.* Just before these words Paul told the Colossian (3:15 & 19) husbands to love their wives, and do not be harsh with them. He told them to let the peace of Christ rule in their hearts for they were called to peace. It is a cowardly, and an ungodly thing to use physical force to suppress a spouse.

Peter, a married man, wrote (1 Peter 3:7) that we should treat our wives with respect as they are the meeker partner or our prayers would not be answered. If you are a bully in your home do not expect God to waste His time answering your prayers, while He is busy trying to undue the hurt you have caused your bride.

Read: Proverbs 25:28; Colossians 3:15 and 19

Pray: *"Lord, make me and my hands an instrument of your peace."*

Beware of love

Found in a teenage boy's text book was this poem, "Love is like a little lizard it curls up around your heart and then jumps into your gizzard". We laugh as we see displays of *puppy love* not understanding that it is real to the puppy. The kids may not know that it can lead to a dog's life at times. Inexperience in relationships may cause unsafe actions, and plans which might create disasters in the future, so beware in some of the risky areas of love.

When an *attack of love* hits, it may render a person insane for a time period. It can cause a person to swoon and act irrational. We look back now with a smile as we recall the kooky things we did when we were crazy in love.

Sometimes this is no more than new hormones or historionic chemistry which affect our responses. They complicate our rational mind with irrational feelings that lead to silly actions. Someone has said, "Being in Love is kind of like being insane." That might not be far from being correct if you are talking about the being in love stage. When a person tells me they have just fallen in love; I hear those words, and remind them that you fall into a ditch you do not fall into love. If love is to be lasting, and not just a fleeting fancy of emotions, then there needs to be some thought put in the process. Some marriages fail because they were built on a weak foundation. A marriage that fizzles out before the finish may have had a fatal flaw from the first.

Grades will often go down when this enigma hits a person while still in school. Job performance may taper off. They just can not keep their minds on target. This might seem normal, and necessary at first, but it is usually regretted if it continues into their future life. Therefore, think long term. Provide the best *you* for them, and do not smother one another. Come up for air, and allow the object of your affection to breathe. Too often fear of losing a person causes a relationship to progress too quickly, and warning signs of caution are ignored. We might not want to see what is obvious to others because we wish it were not true. Unfortunately, after the wedding is over, all the hazardous waste is still lingering around to cause problems.

Marriage is an institution but so is prison. Who wants to live in an institution? If there are issues which alarm you now, then think twice before making a commitment that you want to last a lifetime.

Love is blind. It is blind to the differences that may cause stress in the future. It is natural for love to want to be blind. Each blind spot should not be a deal beaker which causes you to eliminate every candidate that is lacking in some area, or to which you find different to your own views, or you could die a bachelor, or an old maid. Do talk about variations in style, goals, economics, ethnicity, religion, politics, culture, nature, or any area that appears different. If there are major variations which make other outside people seem to be hesitant or resistant to your relationship; then at least have the good sense to examine the differences realistically. You may be too love blinded to see storm clouds on the horizon, where friends or parents can detect a possible tornado. The prospective of others who are not entwined in the romance may be helpful, if you will listen, and consider their input.

Read: 2 Samuel 11 and 12

Pray: *"Maker of Heaven and Earth, you made me so protect me from harm, even harm from myself."*

Jealousy is cruel and rewarded

There is a strange dichotomy in the Scriptures when it comes to what *jealous* means. It is vital to understand both concepts for the good, and bad types of jealousy as we desire happiness, and work toward success in our marriage. Protecting what we say is ours through jealousy may destroy the very thing we say we are trying to protect.

The Bible tells us in several places that God is a jealous God (Exodus 20:5 and a dozen other places), and that He is jealous for us as His people. We believe that our God is perfect, and without sin yet the Bible also states that, *"Jealousy is as cruel as the grave"* (Song of Solomon 8:6), and it is a bad thing to avoid (Psalm 78:58 & 59 & Proverbs 6:34). How can we reconcile both of these statements, when it seems that they are so different as to defy logic? If jealousy is among the works of the flesh (Galatians 5:20), then how can it be consistent with the nature of a Holy God? Understanding this will help us have a mutually blessed marriage.

The first meaning of the word jealous in a dictionary is to be watchful in guarding. Protecting your mate from others who might wish to harm them, or even from them hurting themselves is a reflection of a godly, and constructive type of jealousy. The Lord wants to protect us, and has our best interest at heart. God also realizes that He deserves full devotion from us as His children, and He therefore objects to us maintaining any person or thing in our lives which would interfere with a mutual bond of love between us and Him. God not only deserves our respect, but He also longs for it. He is jealous **for** us.

Carried along in another definition with this positive view of jealousy is the term zeal. We should be zealous in our jealousy when it comes to being the protector of our mate's reputation, attention, affections, and avoiding possible dangerous activities. Guard each other through placing them in a safe harbor of your trust and respect.

To be jealous **of** someone carries the second and a negative meaning of jealous. It can mean to be resentfully, suspicious of rivalry, or envious. When this type of jealousy raises its ugly side, it conveys we do not trust the other person. This is why it hurts so much when a person we cherish displays jealousy, reflecting they do not trust us. We should understand if there are dishonest or disloyal things which we have done in the past which cast a shadow of doubt over our integrity, then we must work to restore confidence. However to always mistrust another person without good reason is as cruel, and unfair as the grave.

If you are guilty of being jealous *of* your mate then stop, and confess this damaging sin. Ask for forgiveness, and seek to change your ways. It may be that you are only reflecting your own hidden transgressions, projecting them onto another, or you may have unresolved issues related to disappointment from a person of trust in your past. Your spouse should not have to shoulder this unfair burden. Seek out professional help from a pastor, or counselor in order to put the past in the past.

Therefore if you want a healthy marriage, then be jealous *for* your spouse and the marriage but never be jealous *of* them.

Read: Exodus 20:5; Song of Solomon 8:6 and Galatians 5:20

Pray: *"God, allow me to aggressively protect my spouse and marriage, without ever coveting, or getting jealous of their greatness."*

Desperate Housewives

A show on television which I have heard enough about to know better than to ever watch it is called, "Desperate Housewives" of some town. The title could be used by many large and small towns because many women are desperate; some are even despicable and detesting. Before we accuse all women, or any woman for that matter, perhaps we should take some wisdom for the Bible book on wisdom called Proverbs.

An unfortunate event happens in many homes not because of the woman there, but because of the supposed man of the house. Men are supposed to be the spiritual leader of the home, and be willing to be sacrificial in meeting the needs of their wives. Unfortunately, some men wimp out, and have failed to meet the spiritual needs of their wife; much less the emotional, physical, and other needs of the bride of their youth (Malachi 2:15 and 16). No wonder many wives are desperate due to neglect. Shame on us men!

Now that I have bashed us men let's take a look at some verses that apply to women. Humorously the writer of Proverbs suggests it might be better living in the desert, or a roof instead of in the house with a quarrelsome or ill-tempered wife (21:9, 19 and 25:24). Maybe that is why God created garages, and man caves so men can find a little rest and retreat.

The author tries to warn simple minded men, who lack wisdom to stay away from immoral women, who smooth talk unsuspecting hormone charged adolescent brained males, but instead to take the advice of wiser parents to avoid smooth talking females with low or no morals (6:20-29). It declares you will definitely get burned. Chapter Nine (verses 13-18) use the imagery of bad and foolish women tempting us to go astray, while the first part of the chapter uses a woman as a metaphor for true wisdom. It says to beware of any woman who is loud, undisciplined, and without knowledge who has nothing better to do than idly sit in her house, and yell temptations at passers by. Many a man can be found dead inside a modern day *Hotel California*. It may be easy to get inside, but you can not easily find your way out.

The actresses from the afore mentioned program might look beautiful on the outside, but you might as well put a sign on them that reads, *"Like a gold ring in a pigs snout is a beautiful woman who shows no discretion"* (Proverbs 11:22). The attractiveness on the outside quickly fades away after some gals open their mouths, and let you know what is really inside their hearts under that cute exterior.

Before I get angry female mobs burning garbage in front of my house; allow me to remind us of the two possible paths for desperate housewives. There are many wise women around who build up their homes, while there are a few whose homes are destroy from within by their own hands (Proverbs 14:1). No study of womanhood would ever be complete without pointing to the 31st chapter of Proverbs, where the role model for every woman and the desire of every man for such a woman is described.

Remember, when God the Father invaded Earth he brought a simple yet sweet virgin girl named, Mary to play a staring role without the need of any man. One definition of the word *desperate* is having a very great and serious need. If both men and women would deeply desire to find, and follow the original plans of God for their lives; then maybe we would not have so many *Desperate Housewives*.

Read: Proverbs 31:10–31

Pray: *"Heavenly Father, grant that I would use wisdom in the role you have placed me, and fulfill my deep desire to please you, and become everything my home needs me to be."*

Beware Water Fountain Romances

It often begins innocent, sometimes from both parties. It seems like a supportive coworker of the opposite sex begins to listen to a general complaint concerning your marriage, or it is a concerned look, or conversation which indicates the other person noticed you acting disconnected. Coworkers are bound to meet at informal times while getting coffee, or at the water fountain. There may be lunch breaks, and before, or after normal work hours business meetings, when conversation start to cross over into our personal lives or problems.

This always seems innocent at first, and is never intended to become improper; but it can, and does happen. Situations begin to fall into gray or compromising areas. There are some people in positions of authority, or predators who look for an easy way to satisfy their own lusts, and selfish goals, that also extort these times of vulnerability, which we face at times in our marriages.

It appears that this phenomenon is a growing problem in the work place from the direction of both sexes. By the time most of us get to work, we have put on our best faces and clothes, but the real normal us has been left behind at our homes. Some of us do spend a great deal of our lives in the work place with others. Although this does not have to lead to a problem adversely affecting our marriage, it can.

Slowly we may approach a line of danger without ever knowing how close we are coming to it until it is too late, because our emotions are conflicted and confused. We really do not know the other person at work the way we would learn in a normal social dating relationship. Team spirit in the work place; and compassion for our fellowman may lead to hurting instead of helping the other person. As we discuss the problems of our private life; it becomes easy to believe that this new relationship or attraction might be heaven-sent to relieve us of the present stress in our marriage.

Remember if a person does not respect the commitment they made to their current spouse, nor cares about the pain they are afflicting on yours, then what makes you think they will be faithful if you jump ship with them; only to discover that they are headed to a new Port-O-Call after spending some time with you. The brief book of Obadiah has a stern warning in verse 15 which states, *". . . as you have done, it will be done to you. Your dealings will return on your own head".*

My advice is to build a fence at the top of this slippery slope, and not a hospital at the bottom of the cliff where there is a lot of slop. Men should develop supportive friendships with other men, and women should only discuss personal matters with other women. Close accountability partners who are given the right to ask us the hard and personal questions, should always be our spouse or a person of the same gender. The subtlety of Satan who seeks to destroy the beauty of marriage is just too dissipative, deceptive, diabolical, and dangerous to ignore the truth that we live in a fallen world, and anybody can fall into sin.

I realize that as a professional counselor, I have women who come to talk to me in my office. My office with the glass window, where we can be seen by others in order to protect both our testimonies, and where there is a desk which separates me from those I am trying to help. A problem which counselors, pastors, priests, lawyers, doctors, and some others face is how to balance caring support with a failure to insure proper boundaries with those they are trying to help. When I have taught counseling at the college level, all my students are required to read a couple of chapters from an old textbook of mine. It is entitled, *"The problem clergymen do not talk about."* Yes, it is about this issue of crossing the line sexually or inappropriately. It happens more than we want to admit. In these situations three is always a safer number, and stick to your gender that have solid relationships themselves.

Read: Proverbs 27:12; 29:22; 2 Timothy 2:22 and 1 Corinthians 6:18

Pray: *"Protect me Lord, from my own desires to help, and be helped by others, so I do not make an error in judgment which could hurt my marriage."*

Until debt does tear us apart

Since many men are usually the risk takers as their adventuress natures reflect, it makes sense that the wives should take care of the cents. If this sent a scent of unpleasantness to your smeller, then your household may be different than mine. Whoever is deft in making financial decisions, and is the book keeper type in the family should be given the responsibility to be sure debt does not sink the marriage. A wise man does not lose control of leading his home, because he delegates the responsibility to write checks, and balance the checkbook to his wife; if she is better at doing it.

Debt has been humorously defined as, *buying things you don't need with money you don't have to keep up with people you do not really like.* It is never funny when economic pressures are placed as a heavy weight on the home. It is better to eat on a cardboard box, and be happy, happy, happy, than to have a fancy table in the kitchen, but not be able to afford to put food on it without worrying. Proverbs states it this way (Proverbs 15:16 and 17), *"Better a little with the fear of the Lord than great wealth with turmoil. Better a meal of vegetables where there is love than a fattened calf with hatred."* Money can not buy happiness but lacking enough of it can probably bring you misery.

One problem some young couples have is they expect to have in the first year of marriage all the things they saw their parents have after a lifetime of saving and working. Money decisions are difficult to make at times. It really does not matter whether you have a little or a lot, because we typically spend whatever we have. If we have more we tend to spend more. A very wealthy person was asked how much money it took to satisfy a person. His answer was, "Just a little bit more."

We ignore the wisdom of the ants. *"Go to the ant, you sluggard; consider its ways and be wise! It has no commander, no overseer or ruler, yet it stores its provisions in summer and gathers its food at harvest"* (Proverbs 6:7 and 8). Failing to save or plan for the unexpected expenses in life is a formula for disaster. If you spend one penny less than you make then you will survive; but if you spend one penny more than you earn, then eventually misery will catch up with you.

A pattern which is both sound and biblical is to honor God, and give the first 10% of your increase to the place where you worship; set a budget to use the next 80%; and save 10%. This may not be what others are doing, but it proves to be wisest in the long run.

Both parties of the marriage should pool together to make decisions on how the financial resources are to be used. This will soon take the phrase, "I told you so", and other disappointments out of the family conversations. Problems, challenges, and responsibility will then be shared whenever they come up.

Read: Proverbs 6:7, 8 and 15:16, 17

Pray: *"Lord, we thank you that you gave us life, and promised to meet all our needs, so don't let us mess it up. Help us to remember, we are stewards of your blessings, so we thank you for all that we have. Help us to be content with that, Oh Lord."*

Silence is either golden or yellow

There was a plaque hung in my Junior High School boys' gym locker room which read, "It is better to be quiet and thought a fool than to open your mouth and remove all doubt". This is a paraphrase of both Proverbs 13:16 and 17:28. There is a time to speak up and there are times when wisdom counsels us to keep our mouths shut. God gave a message through Zephaniah for all the people to shut up (1:7) when they were before Him. This was because the Lord had seen what they were doing, and He had had enough. It was time for them to listen. Wise is the person who knows when to speak, and when to keep their mouth closed. It is a skill set many of us have yet to develop. It is often difficult to know which is the proper route to take. You must decide in each case what to do without blaming me for your decision.

Some help may be discovered in two verses in Proverbs chapter 26 that are next door to each other, although at first they appear to be in contradiction. Verse four instructs us not to answer a fool, while the next verse tells us to answer a fool. Again timing and situation are vital to consider in deciding which direction we should take.

The first verse warns us that we should not use foolish methods in our communication despite if the other person is doing so. We are just as unwise as a fool if we lower ourselves to use the same destructive verbiage, and tone of a fool who engages or enrages us. The next verse declares we should confront stupidity with the truth, or they will keep on going in the wrong direction. A practical application of both verses might be for a wife to let their husband know you believe they made an incorrect turn, and are going in the wrong direction, but once said, you might as well save your breath, and not add to the conflict. Not to tell them your opinion may be *yellow,* whereas stopping from repeating, "I told you so" is *golden,* and stops short of becoming nagging.

People who suffer from low self esteem, or have had bad experiences with straight forward communication may just clam up, and refuse to say anything out of fear or discomfort. Real love should provide an atmosphere of trust where a married couple should be able to be clear and straight forward to each other, even when they suspect there will be some conflict, if you believe you both can weather the storm. Good marriages often have disagreements, and argue while trying to convince their mate that their opinion is right. Bad marriages may have passed the point of believing the other person can change, or is even willing to listen to them. Not fighting at all may be cowardly, or non-productive, and reflect a stagnate failure in the growth of the relationship. You might have difficulty starting a possibly stressful interaction, if your personality type has low self esteem or is non confrontational desiring to always have people like you. Your silence is your choice, but you must ask yourself; is this not worth risking some discomfort in order to make the marriage better? Weathering the storm might just be refreshing.

Not communicating when you should, may be reflective of an unforgiving spirit. You want to harbor a harmful resentment toward a real or perceived injustice, so you punish that person through the silent treatment by refusing to talk. This usually is destructive. Bring it up, and talk it out, or you run the risk of impairing yourself, and the relationship. Perhaps you are afraid that it could get worse if it comes out in the open. Is this really true, or just a cowardly manner you have of dealing with painful subjects? Being afraid of the response will lead to everything staying the same. Is that what you truly want or just the coward's way out?

If not forgiving a person is the reason for the silent treatment, then you must work on your problem of an unforgiving heart alone before approaching the needed discussion. After you receive confirmation that you can forgive a transgression, it might be that you determine to never bring up the topic at all. In that case silence is golden.

Do you not trust your mate? Is that the reason for your silence? Maybe you are just too tired or lazy to put it the effort to make things better. If this is the case then do not blame your spouse, who you think might have a problem, while you remain quiet, and allow things to deteriorate. Withholding relevant information as a way of controlling others reflects your distrust of that person. In this case silence is yellow and not golden.

Please understand that if you believe talking about an issue could lead to a destructive or dangerous situation, then you should take the discussion to a place where it would be safe. Around spiritual leaders, at a counselor's office, a police station, or in the presences of someone you both trust, and could contain the situation might become a safer environment to be boldly open. Timing is also vital. The first fifteen minutes in from work; after a period of other stress; or when physically, or emotionally drained is poor timing, and an unwise decision for having difficult discussions.

Read: Proverbs 13:16; 17:18, 28 and 26: 4, 5

Pray: *"Lord, help me to speak up and to know when not to speak."*

The One way group

"It's my way or the highway," is what some people say or think. This philosophy limits both the diversity and the creativity to just one brain. People like this have never come to the realization that two heads are better than one. Quite frankly they do not even have one brain to think with because they are so ego driven and closed minded, that they are ignorant of their own limitations. They will no doubt stop reading about here, because they are clueless that this section might be about them, and could help them.

It is usually husbands, but it can sometimes be wives who think with this limited perspective. Some real macho men believe they are such the master of their own fate that it is beyond their comprehension that God gave them a wife to broaden their possibilities and enhance their limited abilities. If you are married to such a person, then you have my condolences along with the sympathy of most of the rest of the World. Be assured the Lord sees your situation, and will reward all your suffering.

Perhaps it might be like what confronted Post-exilic Judah (Ezra 4-6) when those who thought they knew what was best for everybody sent a letter to the Persian emperor Xerxes. Their letter was filled with lies, but it still stopped the work of rebuilding temporarily. A famous quote can be applied here, "A lie can travel around the World while truth is putting on its shoes." It has been used by Winston Churchill, who got it from James Callaghan, and was also used by Mark Twain. Before any of them used it, Charles Spurgeon used it. Later in Haggai's day a similar group tried the same tactic, sending a letter to King Darius. It really backfired on them when the enemies of truth are required to help finance the rebuilding of the Temple which they had tried to stop.

It may do you little good to confront this issue straight on, unless your mate has a weak moment, or finally comes to their senses, and asks for your input. Maybe they might find this article lying around, and ask what you think. A good script for you might be to point out that others have the same challenges, and some have been able to grow out of it.

This form of sin is sometimes magnified with those who suffer from bi-polar disorder, because in a manic stage they feel they are invincible, and can do no wrong. A mental health profession would be of great help in this area.

For others, it is not that simple because, *nobody is as blind as the person who refuses to see.* Some men may insist on having everything done the way they feel is best in spite of the responsibility being rightfully under the other person's influence or arena of control. You might console yourself in remembering when they say it is my way or else to God, they will always lose that battle. God has a way of humbling the proudest people in very public ways. The statements, *"How are the mighty fallen?"* (2 Samuel 1:19) for individuals, and for a group (Revelation 18:10) remind us that fame is fleeting, and power/control is always temporary. The pages of Scripture are littered with great people who fail and fall because of their own inflated self worth. (Read Daniel 4:28-37.)

People in the one way group all have the same problem, pride. Proverbs (16:18) warns *"Pride goes before destruction, a haughty spirit before a fall."* Turn to Isaiah 14:12-17, and see how a mighty king is compared to Satan. Both of them, along with many others discover that placing too much emphasis upon being in control of everybody else is a sign of pride which has slain multitudes. Beware, if you find yourself among the *one way* group for it eventually leads to being totally in charge of only your own little small world, and being very lonely.

Read: Deuteronomy 9:27; Judges 2:19; 1 Samuel 15:23 and John 14:6

Pray: *"Enlarge my ability, and understanding oh Lord to include the wisdom of others."*

Marriage Stalemates

In the game of chess there is a point at which no person can win, and therefore a decision is made to call it a tie, and maybe just start a new game. It is sometimes declared when only the two opposing kings are on the board alone, without any means to make any progress toward winning the match. In those cases as in some marriage disagreements nobody wins. The good news is that nobody loses either.

For some couples, when they see there is no way to resolve an issue, they determine that a divorce is the only way to handle it. If a marriage unit is mature enough for both parties to be honest to each other, and at the same time to not be able to come to a positive conclusion or compromise, then maybe a *Marriage Stalemate* should be declared. I describe this as both couples agreeing to disagree.

If the wife has told the husband her opinion of the correct way to turn while on a family drive, and he still does not agree, then maybe she should pull back, and wait for hubby to get to the dead end, and to admit he was wrong. My sweet wife has used this method at various times. She allows me to be the head of the house (this is the way the Bible says it should be), and to fall on my face at times, because she knows that if I never make mistakes, then I can not learn from them. She normally does not say, "I told you so" too much. An arrogant husband who never listens to his wife's suggestions is failing to use 50% of the resources which God has placed at his disposal. There is a classical theological term for such men. It is 'BOZO.'

Anything with two heads is a freak, but this is not permission from the Scriptures for a man to be a dictator. Both husbands and wives should have a predetermined area of influence which is totally under their control. We can assist each other with the other person's responsibilities, but not take over unless requested to do so.

Going to another room to cool off might allow for clarity and calmness in the discussion at a later, less stressful time. Being creative can also help. One preacher I know solved all their family vacation problems by going to separate vacation spots. Who says you always have to walk together in the same direction all the time?

When talking it out won't work, it might be wise to call in a neutral third party. This can be almost anybody who is not viewed as bias, has good sense, and is trusted by both parties. It should be agreed upon in advance that the outsider's decision is final, before each person tells the arbitrator their side of the issue.

There should be a reset key in some marital strife situations. Throwing the baby out with the wash water, or biting off your nose to spite your face seems wastefully destructive for people who watch as well as the self-appointed punisher. If you have spent so much energy in bringing your marriage together and forward before this boiling point; why throw it all away now? Have you not looked forward to see that in ten years or sooner, that many transactions will be regretted, but it will be too late, if you have a knee jerk reaction or over react in a stupid manner now. Ask yourself if this had not gotten started, and brought us down to this low point then what would we be doing instead? Perhaps ask yourself, what advice would you give to a friend if they had this same impasse?

Sleep on it, and tomorrow pretend it never happened when you wake up. When all else fails to get you an answer, then wait until further light comes. Have the courage and wisdom to say that this is one fight neither of us will win so let's pretend it never happened, and call a stalemate.

Read: Proverbs 14:16; 22:3 and 27:12

Pray: *"God, some fights are just not worth fighting. Help us to realize our marriage is more important, than winning an argument."*

Much to do about the Kids

Parenting advice from a singing preacher

The poetic book of Psalms has been beloved by many cultures over a long period of time. A few of those recorded among the 150 Psalms may be as old as Moses, while most have come from King David about 3,000 years ago. It is there we find pretty songs, poetry, prayers, promises, prophesy, as well as previous history, and practical advice. The writer of these chapters seems to be a poet, preacher, prophet, and a singer.

Two Psalms (127 and 128) have a particular focus for the family. It is to that aim that we direct our attention to learn important lessons from the past which benefit us parents today. These are among fifteen songs called, *Songs of Ascent* which were sung as people came into the city for annual national worship experiences. Some believe a choir stood upon the Temple stairs to chant their words, or were used by individuals as they climbed the fifteen external steps. These two Psalms begin by reminding families of the futility of our efforts if we fail to allow the Lord to establish, and direct our homes. Many parents of teenagers might be encouraged by the reprieve to trust your children, and go on to sleep instead of getting up early to fret, laying down in fear, or worse yet staying awake in order to worry, until they get in the door. God provides us with the ability to sleep in peace, if we have instilled into our kids a proper godlily perspective which can guide their actions.

The text declares children are the gift from God as they are called a reward not a punishment. Although most parents at times do feel like their teenagers are a punishment, for what we inflicted upon our parents, when we were teenagers. Each is a unique individual, and at some point all are sent out of the home like an arrow targeted for greatness. Until they are sent forth, they are to be grouped together in our quiver like home, and protected by their owners. It is a blessing to have your quiver full (my wife and I have a # 3 quiver expanded to include 5 grandkids). As verse five states, we are proud of them all, and both parents and children are glad to be classified together as family, no matter to whom we are talking.

Our next chapter starts to inform godly households that they are blessed because we have walked in the footsteps of the master designer. Parents dare not create an alternate path other than following God's directions for raising their family. All necessary provisions will be given to us due to our honest labors. Happiness and health are granted to us. Our wives will remain close by our side as we team together in child rearing responsibilities in our prosperity, while the children surround us like little twigs growing around the roots of a mighty olive tree. Our prerequisite is simply to trust God with reverential fear as a type of worship, and then to enjoy the bounty of a secure home.

The chapter closes by including a prayer of blessing as your neighbors, and community are favored by your proximity until the end of your days. We are promised we can look forward to watching our grandchildren growing up in a time of peace throughout the nation. I like what this guy wrote.

Read: Psalms 127 and 128, before you read this section

Pray: *"May we trust you as parents during the time you have loaned us our children, so we might instill within them the inner joy and wisdom, which you have provided for us."*

A Family Council

Whether you are a unit of just two, or you have been blessed with many more, this communication method helps weather storms of difference and even defiance. This simple tool for discovering resolutions to quarrels may be especially true, if there are teenagers in the house, who have begun to test the limits, and patience of their parents.

Two main complaints I hear from children is that they do not think their parents ever listen to them, and they do not feel they ever have their day in court where they can speak their mind, because the system is 'sooooo' unfair. The following are some simple ways to eliminate that contention.

A family council is a time during the week where any individual or group may call a meeting of the whole family (that should include everyone living in the home), where petitions may be presented, and problems can find solutions. They should be held in the best location for comfort, and neutral conversations (preferably not an office or bedroom of a parent). The television, MP3 players, computer games, cell phones, and all other distractions must be turned off. A set time, and day of the week should be selected in advance, which allows an hour of the most uninterrupted space. Less time may be necessary if small children are involved, but there probably should be a limit of about an hour for any age. Only one issue is to be brought up in a family council event. No wandering into unstructured side streets, previous frustrations, or failures, and dead end alleys.

Whoever calls for a family council gets to have the floor first, and presents the entire issue, before any one else tries to shoot them down. The issue may be one as simple and noninvasive as, "Where are we going for vacation?" It may be as volatile as, "I want my boy friend to move into my bedroom".

Native American Indian cultures had a similar plan. At the council fires where group information was sought, they often used a talking feather stick. This method allowed the voice of even a small child to tell the others where he saw the buffalo. This vital information would have been ignored by the adult leaders, if it were not for the use of the talking stick. My wife bought me one for my counseling practice. This rule is simple. Whoever has the stick gets to have the floor, and everybody else must wait their turn. After a person is finished speaking, they lay the stick down which allows another person to pick it up. Others can not answer your questions until you lay the talking stick down. Also, remember it must hit the table. There is no grabbing the talking stick away from another person. An ink pen or wooden spoon works just as well. I do not recommend using a sharp knife.

Gary Smalley has another tool that really works well. He called it the McDonald's theory of Communication. If you have ever gone through a fast food drive-through you know you speak into a box. The box answers back your order. You say something like, "I want a Big Mac and small Fries." The helpful voices repeats, "You want a Happy Meal and some chives?" You say, "No. No!" and try to repeat the order until they get it right, and say what you just said to them.

Many arguments occur because we answer questions which have not been asked, although we are sure we heard the speaker correctly. This frustrates the other person, and causes them to believe you are not listening, and have changed the subject. McDonald's Theory allows you to repeat what the other person has said. This accomplishes two helpful results. The other person believes you really do listen to them, and it gives you a longer time to decide how you should answer. Anybody feels better, if they realize they are so important to you, that you really listen to them. Steven Covey states in *Seven Habits of Highly Effective People*, "seek to understand before you seek to be understood."

I will warn you in advance that the *Talking Feather* and *McDonald's Theory* will make a ten minute conversation two hours long, so you may not always want to use them all the time. It will however cause the volume and yelling to lessen. The reason most people raise the volume level is because they are trying to speak louder than the person who they want to hear them, who is also speaking at the same time. Typically, in many disagreements, we just do not hear each other correctly.

It may go like this. A wife may have three questions to ask her husband. After the first question, a good husband will try to answer the question, but meanwhile the wife is going on with her second agenda which the husband has not heard, because he is still trying to get out his answer to the first of his wife's questions. The man may not be effective with good communication skills, but is sure that he had better say something, or it will appear that he is not listening. They continue getting louder, because they both believe it is important to be heard.

By the time she gets to her third issue, she is at the top of her volume capacity, while the husband is still elaborating on the first point, and trying to allow his ego not to be bruised by explaining why his way was really best in the first place for all concerned. This means he never heard the second and third questions, which were really the most important ones to her. She just needed to get the first one out, so she would not forget to include it.

By now the husband has finished his explanation, which he is sure his wife should agree with, but which she never heard due to the fact she was busy correctly wording her second and third points. Not only does he not get credit for its brilliance, but he does not have a clue what the last two questions were all about, and his wife is now mad, and convinced the he just does not listen to her, *ever*. They are both hoarse from yelling, and anything they had planned for the evening is now undoable. All this can be complicated, because a child has interrupted the conversation, and neither mate remembers where they left off, or what they actually have said out loud because they rehearsed it so many times in their minds already.

A family council is not the only method to resolve family struggles, but it can be productive, fun, and train children in proper problem solving techniques. It may just be the favorite memories of a healthy family, who know how to work through issues together as a team.

Parents should trust their children not to have all the answers, but to come up with good questions. Children should be made to feel they are important by knowing their parents will listen to them. Also, remember the golden rule here: "He who has the gold makes the rules." This means that parents or the landlord still must make the final decision, but at least all parties realize that they had their shot.

Read: Acts 6:1-5 and 15:1-22

Pray: *"Jesus, help me to really listen to others in my family with the same energy I want them to use when listening to me."*

The imperfect family

If there ever was a family which should have been established on a solid foundation; it should have been that first family of Adam and Eve. It contained many of the ideal situations which some of us wish were our own.

They began their lives living in a perfect garden called Eden, where there were not threats or competitions. Eve could never compare her husband, Adam, to her previous boy friends abilities or good qualities. Adam would never be able to say he liked his mother's cooking better than Eve's meals. The job market was wide open, and there were no distractions like telephones or televisions to interrupt communication.

If you have read the story in the Bible, then you know that they both blew it by sinning, and each marriage since then has had to deal with male stubbornness, and females being subtle or naive. Before, it was fun to work, and pain, even in childbirth was not an issue. What happened was Satan (the serpent tempter) attacked on three fronts just like he does today. The fruit from the tree in the midst of the garden was good to eat, pleasing to the eyes, and would make you wise. In our day temptations come in those same three categories of the lust of the flesh, the lust of the eyes, and the pride of life to take us away from God's perfect plan for us.

Their first two boys ever born could not even live together in harmony. From them came the first murder. This family dispute may have been the first war over worship style. This focus on competition with each other is reflected in other early case studies in Scripture.

The patriarchs, Abraham and Sarah, hatched an idea they felt was solid. Unfortunately, it leads to two half brothers, Isaac and Ishmael, who are still fighting today as Jews and Arabs. Isaac's twin sons, Jacob and Esau, started fighting in the womb, and continued through out their lives as they lied to and fought each other. Jacob had twelve sons. That sounds wonderful except they were from a very dysfunctional blended family. Jacob married two sisters (at the same time), had two mistresses on the side, and fathered children with all four. You think your family life is tough? Wouldn't you like to be part of their family reunions? Jacob also was cheated by his father-in-law, and in time treated him dirty as well. It appears that God had some pretty hard people to work with in that day.

One of those brothers from father Jacob was sold by some of the other siblings to a slave trader, and then they lied to their Dad about it. You think that lying to parents is new? Because of Joseph's forgiveness, and the brother's repentance they lived happily in Egypt after surviving a famine in their own land. Times got worse in the next 400 years until God prepared, and sent a Moses to save the day for the people of God.

Still this family with all these issues went on to established the nation of Israel. God's selected people Adam and Eve, who started it all may have made mistakes, but I for one am glad they stayed married. So maybe your family can make it too.

Read: Romans 5:12; 1 Timothy 2:13, 14 and 1 John 2:15-17

Pray: *"Thank you God that you can do great things with people, despite what material you have to work with."*

Children are Complications and Completions

Children are both complications and completions at the same time. If you want children to ward off a divorce, and think that having a baby will turn your problem marriage over into a good one, then you need professional help. Not only are you seeking to have a child for the wrong reason, but that can only complicate things more, and you will have selfishly placed an innocent child right in the middle of problem issues. The only time having a child will solve a marriage problem is if you both are upset that you do not have one.

The Old Testament prophet, Micah has some interesting reminders. Although he could not have known first hand, he mentions the pain and agony of birthing a child (4:10). He also alludes in the First chapter (verses 8 and 16) to the lament of raising children to the point of wanting to pull your hair out. That makes echoes in my memory of hearing my Mom say, "Come here, and I am going to yank every hair in your head out." This did not usually motivate me to want to run to my mother!

During some marriage seminars we play a game where we time how long it takes for a person to walk across the room by themselves. Next, we give that person a spouse to hold hands, and traverse across the room. That takes longer. Then, we place another person inside their arms with one hand on each of theirs, and observe how awkward it is to make progress to the opposite wall. By the time we allow that child to stand up, and add a couple more children (adults) in the circle it becomes hilarious. It is especially true when the adult playing a teenager is trying to break out of the family circle, and go in a different direction. I am sure you get the picture. Having children will complicate your marriage. Sometimes complications make life exciting or at least interesting.

I become angry when television commercials present having children as an inconvenience. So please do not think I am against couples reproducing. Nothing is as natural, and normal as it is for the Lord to bless a home with new life. Sometimes babies may be born before we think we are ready *but ready or not* they often come as a natural byproduct of our love, or perhaps our lust. Some of you may read this section, and wonder why God has not answered your prayers, and allowed you to have a healthy pregnancy. Unfortunately, I am not capable of giving you a satisfactory answer except to encourage you that God really does know best, despite how unfair life might seem at times.

Children can also be viewed as completions to our lives. Some work which was begun by the parents may be completed by their offspring. We should not reproduce for the purpose of having free labor to finish the tasks we begin, but it does happen at times. It is not unusual for a parent to want a better or easier life for their children, than they had as they grew up. Most parents do work in order to provide a better platform for their children. Wanting something better for our families has motivated many parents to sacrifice themselves to supply the family's needs. None of this is new. It can be seem in the pages of Scripture, and modern day life.

When we look at all of human history; we are able to notice the progression of Almighty God, who instructed the first couple to fill the Earth with their offspring. A careful study of Scripture reflects a development of the Lord revealing His program of redemption for humanity; and establishing righteousness, and justice throughout the globe. To raise a child in godliness is to cooperate with God's intended purpose for life and procreation.

Read: Ephesians 4 13; Colossians 2: 9-10 and 4:11-12

Pray: *"Lord, these children are your gift to us for a brief time. Please help us point them it the direction you planned, and allow them to find complete fulfillment in your plan."*

Tailoring your kids, and leaving a legacy

Two gifts every parent should desire to give to all their children are *roots* and *wings*. Genetic codes are already written within the embryo of each child at conception. Intellectual, moral, spiritual, emotional, and other factors are the nourishment we invest in our children as they grow. Both heredity and environment are important. The question is not whether nature or nurture is most important. They both are important, but after birth you can only control the environmental structure. Healthy roots are what you as a parent provide.

Child psychology teaches that as children develop they go through various stages. Each has their own set of challenges. To *tailor* your child means investing your time, resources, and energy in an unselfish manner to provide the personal equipment needed for the child to become a complete, and healthy functionally independent adult at some future date. I have never had a tailor made suit but being measured for a tuxedo was bad enough. It made me feel uncomfortable with an invasion of my personal space. Working to help your child be suited for their future may be uncomfortable for both parties at times, but it is necessary to acquire a proper fit. It must take into account both the uniqueness of the individual being suited, and the abilities of the mature professional.

The Scripture encourages us, *"To train up a child in the way they should go."* A parent is instructed to direct the child through positive and negative means to help them discover who they are, and who they can become. This means we should study how God made them, and listen to what both they, and God have to say about how they are to act, and where they should end up.

Some helpful hints for adults are to remember they are children, and not just a little one of us adults. They do not have our experience or our hang-ups. They are a little them who will be a big them one day. A member of a previous church said, "They will still be mine when they are 99." She was right. We will always be their parent, but they should be allowed to develop *wings* of their own someday. Our home is a launching pad for their future home, usually in a different location. It is unfair to try to relive our lives through them. We had our chance, so let them become whatever God intended for them to be.

Be friendly to you kids, but be sure to be a parent first. If necessary, do not be afraid to *not* be their friend. They can always get friends, but they often need a parent more than they need another friend as stupid as they are. Adult parents should not bring themselves down to what ever childish temper tantrum is being thrown. You are an adult, so act like it, and stay in control of your emotions. Keep your eyes on the goals you have for them, but respect that they have goals of their own.

Always reflect the righteousness of God as well as His love and mercy. Try to end your relationship with them well as they enter adulthood. We could all take a lesson from King David who passes the baton of building the Temple to his son Solomon with words of encouragement, and support as it is found in 1 Chronicles 22 and 28. Support their dreams without interfering with them. Let them fly as high as they can, but be willing to catch them if necessary. Be sweet, and remember they will probably pick out your nursing home.

To be honest with my readers, "I wanted to write all these words of counsel for our adult children, and grandkids with the hope that they would be able to build upon everything I have learned, and not make as many dumb mistakes as I have."

Read: Proverbs 22:6 and 23:12-19

Pray: *"May we as parents give all our children the special foundation they need, and may you help us at the right time to set them free to become everything you intended them to be. Thank you God for giving us this vital task."*

The Children left behind after Divorce

Two things I can tell you about children whose parents divorce. If your marriage has already died, and the divorce is final then you may be reading this too late. These words are not meant to add another burden of guilt upon that which you may already be carrying. Perhaps, it may help you realize what you have been facing is not out of the norm for the children of divorce.

Before we go further allow me to ask you which natural disaster do you think is the most damaging to emotional health? Floods, fires, lightening, earthquakes, tornados, hurricanes, tsunami, and others are all horrible experience to try to live though. But what is the one which creates the most fear to our emotional health?

I believe it is the earthquake. They have no warning; it shakes your very ground of being, and there is really nowhere to run, and escape the devastation. The ground of Earth is supposed to stay still so we can function normally. When the foundation you depend upon for security shakes, moves apart, and reveals distaste for each other, then you start to question where to run for safety. Parents provide stability for children.

In the time of a flood you can head for higher ground, except for Noah. Normally in a flood there was rain somewhere either where you are or up river. The same is true about lightening strikes. Lightening is scary, and the noise of thunder afterward makes most of us jump. Still, there is some kind of warning, if you look at the sky, or listen to the weather channel.

Heat from a fire and its smoke motivates most sane people to flee from it to safety. Weather patterns are becoming more predictable with the advances in metrology, and our televisions track possible dangers of tornados and hurricanes. When an earthquake strikes, it is without warning. We become so mundane over the possibility of an earthquake thinking the ground will always serve us consistently as a place to walk or drive. We even build huge cities on fault lines. My thoughts are that all Californians are craze to live out along the San Andres fault, until I remember that we can fish in Reel Foot Lake as a result of a monster 1810 earthquake in Kentucky and Tennessee.

Parents are the stabilizing ground for children. They are older than their children, and except for when we are teenagers, we function as if parents are smarter than we are. One of the healthiest things we can do for the family is provided a stable and secure foundation for them. Tests have shown that a child's healthy self esteem is established more through believing their parents care about each other, than if they believe the parents care about them. It goes back to a safe place to stand on.

The rationalization that we are harming our children by staying together and not being happy is a convenient excuse that does not hold water. One thing which is true is the children are still better off in a dysfunctional family, rather than two dysfunctional families in different locations which they have to share. If you really believe you have a bad marriage which is doing harm to your children, then get some help, and work on the marriage to make it functional.

One issue that is almost consistent among all children of the divorced is the kids blame themselves for the break-up. Adult worlds realize the reality of failure. But for a child seeking to grow up into an adult, like their parents, believes they have no hope. If big people can not keep their promises, and fix broken things, then their little minds reason what hope do they have. Besides a child's world revolves around themselves so if they had been a better boy or girl then there would not have been pressure that caused a break up of their parents. If a divorce does occur be sure to reassure them of your love for your child (children), and clearly declare the division was not their fault.

Another almost universal standard for children of divorce is that they would put their parents back together if they could. It would just be a lot simpler, and they would not have such disrupting lifestyles. Sadly the facts are that about the middle of 2010 half the children in American are no longer being raised by both parents in the same home. They are not going to say this bothers them to the parents because they are still trying to not hurt them. Children do tell counselors these things when parents are not around.

We wonder why the youth culture appears to not have a solid foundation, yet the very home they stand on has had a tectonic shift of their foundations. If what we do in moderation our offspring will do in excess, then our nation is headed for crumbling.

Read: Psalm 11:3 and Jeremiah 12:5

Pray: *"Please protect our children Lord, and do not allow our problems to be taken upon their little shoulders."*

Blended families can be the best or the worst for children

When any family with children is devastated by divorce it is never the original desire of God, but it does not take Him by surprise either. This new way to group families may be hard to pull off successfully, but it is possible, and can be made easier if biblical, emotional, and socially sound policies are followed. Blended families is the term given to any family where there are children from a previous marriage (or almost marriage) brought into a new family unit due to remarriage of either the mother or father. The Bible includes the stories of many blended families which reflect both good and bad results.

Children are not pieces of rope to be used with a selfish agenda to be yanked upon by either side as a way to punish the other once related adult parent. Nor, should children ever be placed in a situation where they are called upon to be a detective to spy on the other 'X' person.

Neither are children pawns to be used to gain money from the other parent by using a pity ploy. If you have every done this then repent immediately, and never do it again. Confess to some adult who will keep you accountable to *cease and desist* such potentially damaging behavior. These are children for Pete sake not your tools/toys to be manipulated.

If actual crimes are being committed against the child, then allow the court system to do their job, and do not take the law into your own hands. It is just too easy to permit your selfish ambition to be spiteful to your 'X'. Lady Justice wears a blindfold to reflect that justice does not play favorites, and is therefore, impartial and fair. Perhaps all concerned parties can get a neutral mediator to resolve the stress, and come to a healthy resolution. Some of the most difficult, dangerous, and saddest counseling sessions I have lead have been with vulnerable children over these issues where the children are used as physical or emotional footballs. Their tears are usually done in private, because their love for mommy and daddy causes them to protect these ungrateful adults. I often wish the adults were as considerate.

Blended families may include children who may be either *his, hers, or ours.* A hard rule to abide by for both parents and children is that whoever is the mom or dad of the house is also the mom or dad over all little ones in the home. Parents rule, and a united front should always be reflected by the adults in that household despite whom was the biological factor in the original birth. Having two sets of rules for each different house, or even in the same house with biological and non-biological relationships is difficult for the kids, so if the warring parents can agree on a standard set of rules, curfews, standards, etc. for both houses, then it is always better for all concerned. If you are the child with two different sets of guidelines, then you still must obey the parents of the house you are in at that time.

Making the best of a bad situation is a part of life. Learning how to accept things which can not be changed, and seeking to correct things which are under your control is important. Life may not seem fair but since 2010 the number of children living in homes without both biological parents is equal to those who do live with their biological mother and father. Parents for your children's sake, and for Christ's sake do not be selfish. Learn to share the children with both parents at graduations, holidays, weddings, funerals, and times of illness. Jesus said it best, *"Do unto others what you want them to do to you."*

Read: Genesis 49:1-28 and Proverbs 24:16

Pray: *"Oh God, cause me to only do what is your will, and help me to never do more harm to my child."*

Letting them fly

A preacher wanted to capture his congregation, and instruct them of financial church needs, so he began his sermon by declaring, "This church needs to start walking for Jesus". To which the interactive crowd replied, *"Yes! Let the church walk on."* Feeling like he might have connected he raised the volume to say, "This church not only has to walk but it needs to start running for the Lord." There began to be several *amen's* and people cheered to indicate their desire to let the church run. Nothing succeeds like success, so the preacher reached even louder in his voice to proclaim, "This church not only needs to walk, and run, but it ought to get up, and start to fly". At this point the group exploded with cries of *"Let her fly preacher, let her fly"* and the preacher felt he was at his peak so he'd better close the deal. In a very serious tone the pastor stated, "If this church is going to walk, run, and fly for Jesus then we are going to need some money!" The church building was a little quiet until somebody in the back said, "We better let the church just walk, preacher".

The reality of the presence of children in the home is almost always a temporary circumstance. This is one reason why a couple should continue to keep their relationship of the two of them as the primary one. Research has shown that healthy self esteem in children is developed more by parents reflecting they love each other even more than if the child believes the parents love them. Some time before the children reach forty years old, we are hoping they will be out on their own, and for better or worse (I hope not too worse) a marriage will be back down to just you two the way you probably started out. Therefore, a functional family of two is the most important to nurture, and keep alive.

Parent-child relationships begin by the parent being over the child to protect, provide for, and guide them. The child looks up for this, and gains wisdom, and stability through the exchange. Children continue to increase their freedoms, and their responsibilities until the parents have succeeded in bringing a child into the world who becomes a totally self sufficient adult, capable of making wise choices in life, and taking responsibility for all their own livelihood and mistakes.

The *Golden Rule* should apply in this developing drama. That means he who has the gold makes the rules. When you can pay all your own bills, then you can make all your own decisions. This means if parents are helping pay for college; they also get to see the grades. If you do not work at your study for college, then mom and dad are not paying for you to party! Freedoms and responsibility should always be tied together. There needs to be no new freedoms without new responsibilities. This is how the real world works, and it is important to teach it all along the road of maturity. If you as a teenager want more freedom, then go to your parents and ask, "What more responsibilities can I have so I can earn more freedom?" Parents who wish for more responsible children must be willing to increase the corresponding freedoms. The goal is to reach a level of total freedom with total responsibility.

Two roadblocks arise at the stage when the little baby birds are ready to fly forth from the nest. One is that the children refuse to take responsibility for their own lives. They are not dumb. They like parents paying all their bills. The other side may also restrict the natural process of things when parents refuse to allow their children to grow up with both freedom and responsibility. If you are bailing them out all the time figuratively and financially, then they are not going to become a finished product the way God wanted you to accomplish. Let them fly. After all it is through our failures that we learn to succeed, and thorough trying on our own that we sense a level of responsibility, that we have reached the marker of adulthood.

It is a great reward to relate to adult children, who have reached the same level of maturity as you. A final stage comes when as a role reversal our adult children become a care taker to their parents, and provide the choice of our nursing home.

Read: Genesis 2:24a; Psalms 127:4; Proverbs 15:20 and 22:6

Pray: *"God, help me to provide both roots and wings for my children."*

Taking your Marriage
to a Deeper Level

The 10 Commandments of Marriage

"Please do not be offended at my adaptation of the Ten Commandments given by God through Moses to Israel, and to us, as it is applied here to the thrust of marriage. They reflect a streamline focus to the target of a healthy marriage."

1. Thou shalt have no other sexual interests and investments in your life. *Friends of the opposite sex are allowed, but avoid close physical contact with anyone to whom you are not married.*

2. Thou shalt not try to remake your mate into your own desired image as a way of trying to have them meet all your needs and expectations. *God did His best in creating them the way they are. Accept them that way, and help them become all that God intended for them to become.*

3. Thou shalt not use the name of your spouse in a condescending manner to impress your friends. *This means at work, over the backyard fence, sewing with friends, fishing, hunting, or any place.*

4. Remember the special days of your relationship in order to celebrate them. *This means do not forget Valentines Day, Anniversaries, and Birthdays.*

5. Honor the commitment you made at the wedding. *You said, "Forsaking all others, keeping your love alive, in good times and bad, whether sick or well, with or without money, as long as you are alive."*

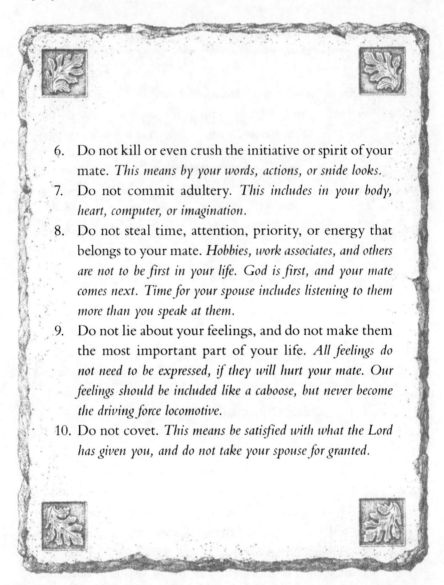

6. Do not kill or even crush the initiative or spirit of your mate. *This means by your words, actions, or snide looks.*

7. Do not commit adultery. *This includes in your body, heart, computer, or imagination.*

8. Do not steal time, attention, priority, or energy that belongs to your mate. *Hobbies, work associates, and others are not to be first in your life. God is first, and your mate comes next. Time for your spouse includes listening to them more than you speak at them.*

9. Do not lie about your feelings, and do not make them the most important part of your life. *All feelings do not need to be expressed, if they will hurt your mate. Our feelings should be included like a caboose, but never become the driving force locomotive.*

10. Do not covet. *This means be satisfied with what the Lord has given you, and do not take your spouse for granted.*

Read: Deuteronomy 5:1-21

Pray: *"Heavenly Father, I am not what I can be in all these areas, and I need your help to do everything I can do to have a healthy marriage. Thank you that I am not what I used to be."*

The magic of please

Some words are so hard to get up from the deep well of my selfish evil heart, and then roll over the tongue only to bust forth from behind the ivory fence I call my teeth, and finally to push their way through my tightly pursed lips. These words named: I am sorry; I was wrong; forgive me; I love you anyway; you are forgiven, and it will never be mentioned again; please; or thank you. It would appear that small words like these are some of the hardest to say; not because of their difficulty to pronounce, but because they are connected to our stubborn wills. Human wills which are often resistant to admit when we are wrong, or believe we will lose something if we utter them.

The opposite is really true. Let us begin being constructive by asking you to reread this article out loud so you can practice saying these words written herein, which are so difficult to verbalize on our own. Start at the beginning again for more practice. For fun, say them in front of the mirror, and watch how the expression on your face reflects whether you look serious when you speak them, or they are painful to the rest of your body. Be sure nobody else is in the room, or you may have the men in white jackets show up at your door. Your family may already believe you are over the edge by even reading this book.

It should be easiest to say, "I am sorry". A person can be sorry that another person hurts even if it is their spouse who pushed your wrong buttons that caused you to do or say what you did, and caused a pain in your mate. You can be sorry they are hurting, even if you are angry or disappointed. If you are not sorry they are hurting, then you've got a big problem buddy. It means you have some weird *get even* complex; or you are a sadist, and enjoy when other people are suffering. Get professional psychiatric help. Are you still reading this out loud? First Corinthians 13 says that real love does not keep score of wrongs committed to them, or try to get even.

Maybe saying, "I was wrong" is the hardest to get out. It impacts our level of self esteem. Prideful or emotionally wounded people may have a harder time with these. You might think if you are honest enough to admit when you are wrong that it will be viewed as weakness, and be exploited. The opposite is normally true, and it is well worth the risk. It takes a mighty big person to admit when they are wrong. Until we admit when we are wrong, then we stall our personal development, and impede the growth of our relationships.

"Forgive me," appears to be such a sweet word. It quickly admits to our being wrong either maliciously or unintentionally through an error on our part. It desires from the other person what only they can give to us. It does not have to be earned, due to the fact it is a gift we desire to receive from them. To fail to include it after saying we are wrong is to be insincere to our admission of a wrong. When you next hear these words addressed toward you, accept them graciously, and respond as quickly as possible with, "I love you anyway, you are forgiven, and it will never be mentioned again" to restore what has been lost by you both. This should immediately heal the breach which had been created.

As kids we learned the magic words were *please* and *thank you*. If we expected to receive something, then the magic words needed to be used. Out of the mouth of babes comes a gem of wisdom. Now practice all the magic words again, and begin to use them often.

Read: Matthew 5:21-25 and Luke 14:7-11

Pray: *"Since I can not change the past when I have failed to use these important words, allow me to begin today to place them in my daily speech."*

Ms. Porcupine meets Mr. Turtle

The imagery fit when I first made up these titles during a marriage counseling session. Many of you have heard about the dance of the porcupine. When it gets cold they try to huddle together to get warm, but after a brief time the sharp pointed quills start to poke their mates, and they retreat away from each other. It is as if they dance close to each other, only after a while to move back apart. There is a fear among some people who are afraid of allowing people to get too close because of past problems, and pain inflicted upon them, when in the past they were struck with the pointed end of their mate's attitude or actions or rejection. This is a natural defense mechanism for porcupines, but it can be counter-productive in developing an intimate relationship with your marriage partner.

Then there is Mr. Turtle who recedes back into his shell and clams up whenever conflict, disagreement, or fear arises in a situation. It is a position of safety but again it does get in the way of trying to bring up issues which need to be addressed. If progress in the relationship is to be accomplished people must exit their shell of safety. Male turtles of the human kind tend to also withdraw whenever they fear being proved wrong.

The gender may be switched, but it seems like women have better abilities to communicate which is why we guys feel like pulling into our shells, due to the fact we believe women have the advantage over us in any discussion. So we may just clam up in a verbal fight.

If you are married to one of these low verbal turtle creatures, then here are four words of advice, "Stop talking so much". It is important that you *learn to listen*. That means you may have to stop talking so much, even though you already know the answers you think your husband wants to say, or the answer you want him to give. You may even have rehearsed your next statements which you plan to say after he gives you his first lame response to your interrogation. Let him get his words out while you patiently wait. Pause, and take a breath before you begin to give a response to his statement. It may drive you crazy, but if you want the reward of better communication, then you need to listen more and talk less. Do not start talking while he is slowly coming out of his shell, or he will retreat back into his safe spot.

The other hint is turtles come out of their shell when they feel safe. Until Mr. Turtle believes it is safe to come out of his shell, and not be attacked by a verbal predator, then he will stay in the safety of his shell. That shell may seen as: be out with the guys until it is too late to have a talk; linger in the garage; hid behind the newspaper; ugly stares; head turned away; zoned out as if the body is there but the brain has been transported to a different dimension; or some other escape tool. Your warmth and developing a place of safety for him may help him be comfortable in launching outside to the real world of open communication.

If you feel you married a female porcupine, then as a man you should be patient as well. This mammal relaxes their quills when they feel safe. If a man approaches such a creature in an argumentative fashion, then expect a defensive posture, and expect to be painfully poked. Words of openness and caring may surprise your wife, if this has not been your typical way of approaching her. Taking the time to understand her fears from the past which created this response will go a long way in you developing the trust she needs, in order to feel secure enough to allow you to get close to her. Isn't that a positive outcome?

Read: Colossians 4:1-6

Pray: *"May we O Lord become better at understanding each other, accepting one another, and overcome the hindrances which have caused us pain and breakdown in communication in the past."*

Love can make you sick

A verse in the King James Version of the Bible, written in 1611 shows us how language has changed over the past 400 years. It says, *"Comfort me . . . for I am sick of love"* (Song of Solomon 5:8). There have been times when I was so tired of hearing about the crushes of my college roommates that I wanted to say I was getting sick of hearing about *their love episodes*. The verse really means the writer was *love sick*. At least that is how we would say it today.

When you are in love, you might stress yourself out to the point that you get physically ill. During stress your stomach muscles may tighten, your neck becomes stiff, adrenalin pumps into the muscles to a point of getting clumsy, perspiration may rise to the surface of your skin, and some other physiological signs may appear. This sounds like an illness to me. There is no medicine you can prescribe for this aliment called love. It was not intended to do this but it can happen. If you are older, then you might hold your breath so long that you turn blue, and pass out, because you are trying to make it look like all that stomach is really in your chest. This is why you ladies should date a guy long enough to force him to exhale in order to see what he is really going to look like in a few years. Men remember that they spend hours getting pretty for a date, and after a few years of marriage they might not look like that in the morning.

When you are sick, everything takes a back seat to your infirmity. When we get a tooth ache all attention is given toward getting some dental relief. It does not matter what is on the schedule it will just have to wait. We must get free of the pain in our mouth. It is sad to me as a counselor, that many people come to me, and tell me that once they had an ache in their heart for their love focus, but now that same person is a pain in another part of their anatomy.

Is there anything that can cure the problem of *love sickness*? Many times the solution is to just get married, so you can always be with that other person through out the rest of your life. This sometimes is a case of the cure being far worse than the disease. In order to stop a virus from getting out of hand, you may need to take a big dose of reality. Thinking with our heads, and not your hormones is a good start. This has never been normal for young people. Do not deny your feelings, because they are real. Do however use your intelligence to look long range, and balance your time, and thought life with other realities, or priorities in life. If you have a short term sickness, then it will pass on, and you will be healthy again. If it lingers long, then take notice because it might only be healed by the medicine of a wedding band.

Perhaps placing in your thinking patterns about what you can give to this other person is vital to bringing down the fever of heated passion, and raising the level of long term goals and commitment. What do you realistic want your future together to look like? Never allow the pressure from the other person to make you sicker. Distance from the source of your infection of affection may help your temperature decrease. This may be the reason many couples back away from each other during engagement for a period of time, to see if they are truly ready for a life time commitment.

The Bible verse above is over three thousand years old so this phenomenon is not new, and will not be going away soon. If you can not get over love sickness, then you will need to live with it until death cures your problem.

It is a good model to spend time with other couples when toxic with love sickness. Double dating is normally a safer thing to do before the wedding. Are there more mature couples who you dream to emulate? See if they are willing to mentor you during your courtship. If the other person wants to privately possess you all by yourselves, then they are either a control freak, or ashamed to be seen out in public with you. See a doctor immediately, or get to an emergency room because you need help.

Read: Song of Solomon 5:8

Pray: *"Lord, help me know if my feelings are real/normal, and keep them in balance with the rest of my life."*

Like, Luv, Lust, and Love

The English language can be confusing to other cultures, because it is such a mixture of different languages, and there are so many exceptions to the multitude of rules. I still have difficulty counting sheep as I try to slip off to sleep, when a sheep is only one, and yet a whole bunch of them at the same time.

We say, "I love my wife"; "I love my pet goldfish"; and "I love Cheerios". I would hope that it is a different type of love for each category, and so does your wife. The New Testament was written in Greek which is a more exact and picturesque language. Greek has seven different words for love depending on the type. Three of those are used in our Bibles. One is a self-centered physical love where we love for what we receive by loving. Another type is a fellowship love between friends. This word is used in Philadelphia. It is a combination of two Greek words. It is the city of *brotherly love*. There are houses and streets in Philadelphia where outsiders are not treated like friends or brothers. The last type of love describes the love God has for us. It is a self-sacrificing love, which He gives to us for the pure joy of giving.

Early stages of what we call love should probably be called *like*. At that stage we find ourselves enjoying the company of the other person because we share common interests, and feel pleasure when we are around them feeling safe. They may even make us feel better about ourselves, or we may sense pride by having them associated with us. We are happy they are with us. This is often called infatuation.

Back in the '60's you could find the word *Luv* scribbled in places. I always believed that meant they had no idea what love was really all about, and since they could not spell it they would not recognize it if real love hit them in the face. It was the Sixties, and we could not spell any more than we could think clear. It was little more than a vague and fleeting emotion based on very little if any commitment. You do not fall in Luv, you fall in a ditch. Relationships built on this lower form of Luv soon dissipated.

The term *lust* might well be described as a selfish physical need being fulfilled without regard, or caring about the object of your lust. Marriages based upon this level will deteriorate unless a more valid type of relationship develops. A marriage based solely on sex, or lust will be reduced in inverse proportion to time, and loss of physical appearance. In time both we and our spouse may begin to lag or sag. My body has the furniture rearranged since the wedding. My chest is now below my drawers. We are to flee from the impulses based on animal, or the carnal nature according to the wisdom of the Bible (1 Corinthians 6:11). Both letters Paul wrote to Timothy warns the youth to beware of this temptation (1 Timothy 6:11 and 2 Timothy 2:22). Lust quickly loses its luster, when lust toward another object to be used, and then discarded, comes along. To take the next step in receiving love you must come to the place of giving love.

This pitfall which distorts our perceptions, and causes us to make a faulty decision as to who we should marry is this confusion over lust and love. They are not the same, even though the terms, and the emotions are often confused together. Lasting love has been defined as, "each for the other and both for God". Love is not defined by what you get, but by what you give. It is difficult to show love until you first have the unconditional love of God invested in you.

Read: Proverbs 27:20; 1 Corinthians 6:11 and 1 Timothy 6:11

Pray: *"Help me to give, and receive love, also to understand the difference early in life."*

Wedded Bliss or Blisters

The dictionary defines "Bliss" as great happiness or spiritual joy. The very next word in my dictionary is "Blister". It carries the meaning: a raised patch of skin filled with watery material caused by heat or an irritation. There is a side meaning of "To lash out with words". An old phrase still used in connection with weddings is, "Wedded Bliss". That is what most married couples expect, and feel when they look starry eyed at each other on their wedding day. Unfortunately, some couples end up thinking that being married to the person they once loved is now just a blister on the hide which brings only irrational. This is not what marriage is intended to accomplished, or is it?

I do not believe we should purposely rub each other the wrong way, until we are left with a tender spot that hurts anytime our mate gets near us. A callous however is similar to a blister, but it serves more to protect us. A callous comes due to that area of our external skin being in contact with another object so many times that it has hardened a place of protection at the point of contact. No other person gets so close to us, and on such a consistent manner as does the person we married, and spend our life with.

About the only time we hear the word bliss is on the day we get married. It is not used in today's normal every day speech. That may be unfortunate, or it might be because married couples soon begin to rub each other the wrong way, until the irritation creates a blister in the relationship, and happiness is sacrificed as the events, words, or lack thereof, fill the space just below the surface of the skin. There it remains, because we may be afraid to examine it honestly ourselves, or poke at it with the sharp needle of discussion.

Almost any contact with the blister will cause greater pain, and causes it to grow while affecting more territory. We may begin to over protect this sensitive spot. Bliss on the other hand grows with each experience which has positive results, and enjoyment as the interaction contacts our lives. The difference between developing a blister and strengthening the skin into a helpful callous comes from two different sources.

We can allow a blister to be created ourselves because we do not hold our marriage close enough, and only allow it to slide through our personality without realizing its painful necessity to our growth. Any person, who is as close as our spouse, will make contact with us in many ways which reveal we are not taking charge of our responsibilities firmly. The blister may hurt because we fail to allow the irritants of daily life to point out a better way of living. If a spouse pricks us by some word or deed, then we may need it in order to correct a bad habit. We may not like them poking us, but we may need it. God brings people who love us into our lives to bless us, and not to bug us, although it is sometimes difficult to know which is taking place. The evangelist Billy Sunday was once criticized for rubbing the cats fur the wrong way by his strong preaching. He replied, "I am doing the right thing, so tell the cat to turn around."

A person may create a blister on us through not being caring to us, or even be seeking to get even, or do us harm. That is their sin, and not your own. Through resisting the natural flow of communication or through insensitivity to our helpmate's feelings, we may be causing a blister instead of a blessing intended to make them a better person. Examine your motives for confronting your mate to see if your words and actions are truly for their good or your own.

Read: Proverbs 27:17

Pray: *"Lord, there is no way the two of us can live this close together without getting in each other's way at times, so help us always be gentle, and helpful to each other. When we feel wounded by the other person allow us to hear that they want us to be all that we can be."*

For better or bitter

Some people go into marriage making a vow to be married as long as no problems arise, and everything keeps getting better and better. The wedding vow states "For better or worse." Few couples do not understand just how worse it can be at times. Most intelligent people realize that the World we live in is not heaven, and that sin affects areas of our lives in a variety of negative ways. There are days in all marriages where it seems to be a lot of *worse* rather than *better*. It may be better off to leave those times out of the diary of your memory. Etch-a-sketch memory is what I call that. Shake your head and forget about it.

Some research on couples before and after marriage has been done to discover which couples will make a successful marriage that will stay together, and which factors are not as important. Unselfish people with healthy habits having learned how a functional family works from seeing it in their family of origin; who have a common goal larger than themselves, like a personal faith; and commitment to God extends hope for the future of a marriage, which will survive the onslaughts of time. A few people find themselves in this category. Most of us common folks must struggle with unhealthy dysfunctions from our past. One cartoon entitled "The National Conference on Functional Families", pictured a speaker with only three people seated in the large auditorium.

Another major factor which holds out hope for a success in marriage for couples are their ability to work through conflict in healthy and a mutually satisfactory manner. All couples disagree at some point. As Dr. Billy Graham says, "If two people agree on everything, then one of them is not necessary." Expect disagreements, it is a natural occurrence among healthy couples. How you resolve conflict is what determines whether you will stay together, and weather the storms of conflict in life.

When couples came to me asking to perform their wedding ceremony, and made statements like, *we never fight*. I tell them it will be my goal in pre-marriage conferences to create a fight for them. Couples need to learn how to resolve conflicts in a productive manner, because they are a natural part of a healthy marriage.

Throwing in the towel and running away at times of conflict is the coward's way out. The verse in Proverbs 27:17 declares, *"As iron sharpens iron so one man sharpens another."* This is really true the closer two people relate. Married couples are the best at knocking off the rough edges of each other as a method God has for causing us to be better people. It takes a hard diamond to cut another diamond. Most of us do not like when the friction of another person rubs us the wrong way. A truthful spouse can become our best coach to assist us to reach our full potential.

God instructed Moses to give Aaron a wonderful prayer of blessing which would be valuable to extend to others, and you might wish it to be extended to you. *"The LORD bless you, and keep you; The LORD make His face shine on you, and be gracious to you; The LORD lift up His countenance on you, and give you peace"* (Numbers 6:24-26).

A wonderful passage in Deuteronomy 11:8-12 promises us the Lord will be with His people no matter what enemies they face. The land of their future is different, than where they did reside, but even there the eyes of God will watch over them, from the first of the year all the way to the end. This land with both hills, and valleys can be like Heaven on Earth for those who discover His secrets of successful living.

Read: Deuteronomy 11:8-12

Pray: *"Lord, allow me to realize you are with me in the valleys of difficulty, and be glorified when we are able to stand tall on the mountain tops of your love."*

Love and Hate

Love and hate both produce very strong feelings, which typically elicit actions on our part. Although we normally place them at opposite ends of the emotional spectrum they may be only a short distance apart. At times they may appear to be two sides of the same coin. When love is rejected from the object of our affections, or when the love we shared is violated in some way, we may flip the coin turning rapidly from love to hate. As violently as we loved a person, we may turn, and say we hate them violently as well.

Two people do not get married claiming to love each other; have 2.4 kids; spend nine years or some amount together; and then reach the point where they desire to end the marriage, because they now hate the person they at one time said they loved, and did not want to live without. Now, they say all sorts of ugly things about each other; hire lawyers and detectives to publicly prove how bad the other person is in order to get a divorce due to the impossibility of working or living together any longer. Unfortunately, it does happen this way all too often.

This topic brings up memories of 1st grade and first loves where *I love you, boyfriend* in the morning turns into *I hate you* before lunch is over. Childhood romances are easy come, and easy go usually without much damage to our personhood. Marriages should be based upon a commitment to work through the storms of life, and not throw the crew overboard at the first signs of stormy weather. Jude (verses 3 and 16) writes that ungodly people are grumbling fault finders who wish only their own selfish lusts satisfied. They only flatter and speak well of others when it suits their vain and self-centered purposes. Jude knew that all people need mercy, peace and love to be multiplied not just added.

One song moans along with, "You always hurt the one you love. The one you shouldn't ever hurt at all." It must have some sound basis in relationships, because it has been recorded by musicians as diverse as Bing Crosby, Connie Francis, Spike Jones, Fats Domino, and Ringo Starr. I did not know such a wide range was possible. Hurting somebody you love is possible because we do not allow a person we do not trust to get close enough to inflict emotional pain on us. Our love interests are allowed to come close within our level of vulnerability. That is why it hurts so badly. We opened the door to who we *at first* thought could be trusted. Then after they hurt us, or disappoint us, or are different than the image we wanted them to be, then our love quickly turns to hatred. If we understand this truth going into a relationship then maybe we will not violate our own sanity, nor place unrealistic standards of behavior onto others. There will be ups and downs in any relationship, but to allow it to reach a stage of vindictive wrath is counterproductive, and borders on the absurd. Love is silly at times, but it should not be irrational or over reactive.

Individuals who suffer from Bi-Polar Disorder, or have abandonment issues because of events in earlier life may be even more sensitive, and over react more than other lovers. This should be taken in consideration, and protective measures put in place. Time heals all wounds, and productive communication before reaching the stage of critical mass is necessary at times for all couples.

The second verse of the above song says, "You always break the kindest heart, with a hasty word you can't recall. So, if I broke your heart last night, It's because I love you most of all." Understanding the reality of marital harmony, dysfunction, and times of stress should create a more balanced approach than flipping the coin so quickly from love to hate. Think before you speak or react. If you have invested time in a marriage, then do not throw it out over a few disappointments. Get professional help from a counselor or clergyman. It never hurts to get an unbiased opinion, or perhaps hire a referee. Take ownership of your part of the problem, even if it is only to admit how unrealistic your past assumptions were, and learn how to work as a team in the process of molding together into a unit which cares about the whole.

Read: Psalm 55:12, 13 and Proverbs 10:12

Pray: *"Grant my love to be long lasting Lord, and help me never violate the trust placed in me by the mate you gave to me."*

If your wife killed you, she would have good grounds

What do you do when you mess up? Change your name; move to another state; or run and hide? Do you get all defensive and make up an imaginary issue to yell against your spouse hoping they will forget your blunder? Or do you get all weepy eyed maybe fake having a terrible illness? It could have been something which came out of your mouth, but not out of your brain. Chances are both spouses will at some time do something really dumb. Oh, you will not mean for it to be boneheaded, and you must have thought it was a great idea at some point, but it is still something which is counter productive to sanity, and your spouse not only finds out about it, but confronts you with what you did. In times like these you may wish to join Nahum (1:7), and take refuge in the Lord and trust Him to be a stronghold in your day (or night) of TROUBLE.

If you are like me there is often *no good excuse* for what you did, and you wish like everything you could call those moments back. People hearing about some silly or risky things I have tried have made the statement, "If your wife killed you she would have good grounds". It does not have to be something as destructive as an adulterous affair. It might be as simple as putting the garbage down for just a minute to answer the phone, and forget for a week that you left it where it would stink up the whole house, while you were gone on vacation. Perhaps it was a sure thing financially, or so the friendly adviser said, which has placed horrible financial stress on your bank account. These are the times we request mercy and forgiveness not justice.

If you botch it up, then fix it if you can. There are sometimes when you try to fix it on your own, and it only gets worse. Reach out for help beyond yourself if necessary. The wise saying states, "don't throw good money after bad."

At some point, every couple needs to learn to just forgive their mate, and put the past in the past. It is always better if the offender learns from their mistake, and changes patterns which lead to the transgression. Some stunts however are beyond repair, and the only redemptive thing which can be done is learn not to ever do it again. It would be easy to continue to bring up these embarrassing topics when you feel the need, but it may damage a relationship which is a mistake as well. Remember we all have some skeleton in our closet which we hope remains there in the dark.

This may be hard to accept, but if you are willing to forgive a spouse their transgression, then not only will you find forgiving grace at a future time, but you will be doing what God has already done for you. No husband or wife is godlier than when they extend mercy to a person who does not deserve it. Read those statements again.

A marriage that has never had some type of conflict which requires undeserved absolution may not believe that after such events a marriage can become an even stronger unit. But this is true. If nothing can be done to change the circumstances, then it may be best to let it slide. You may be wedded to an adventurous soul who constantly surprises you with outrageous activities, but just think how boring your life would be if you did not have all these things to roll your eyes, and shake your head over. It is not what you would have done, but that is why the Lord put the two of you together. Every quarterback needs somebody to run defense for them, so God may be using you to protect the guy running with the ball. Helping the miscalculating partner might bind you closer together in the future, even if you do have a good reason to clobber them. It may be best not too.

Read: 1 Samuel 26:21; Proverbs 12:15; 14:16 and Ecclesiastes 10:12-15

Pray: *"Dear Lord, when I blow it help me to allow my spouse to confront me, and when they mess up help me to meditate on all my flaws before talking to them about theirs."*

Taking it through the Stages

These next ten lines are designed to reflect the possible development which may take place in marriages. I like to call them stages or crossroads.

Marriage goes through 10 Stages

As I have viewed and studied marriages I have seen them transition through particular stages. Below is a humorist reflection of what marriages go through from the beginning to a successful completion.

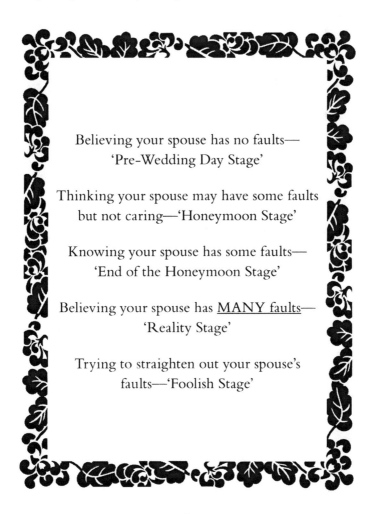

Believing your spouse has no faults—
'Pre-Wedding Day Stage'

Thinking your spouse may have some faults
but not caring—'Honeymoon Stage'

Knowing your spouse has some faults—
'End of the Honeymoon Stage'

Believing your spouse has <u>MANY</u> faults—
'Reality Stage'

Trying to straighten out your spouse's
faults—'Foolish Stage'

Hearing that you are the reason for all
your spouse's faults—'Conflict Stage'

Telling your spouse that they only
have faults—'Really Dumb Stage'

Accepting your spouse with their faults—
'Successful Marriage Stage Begins'

Loving your spouse, and admitting your
own faults—'Honest Marriage Stage'

Believing your spouse has no faults
because you accept them as they
are—**'Completion Stage'**

Read: Ecclesiastes 3:1-14

Pray: *"God, we understand that you are the only unchanging factor in the entire universe so grant us your unchanging mercy, while we grow deeper in our relationship."*

The right order of healthy relationships

Healthy relationships develop over time. There may be love at first sight, but that is usually more an emotional exhilaration that may fly out of your life as quick as it flew into your life. Long lasting love has more to do with commitment than it does with hormonal fluctuations.

First contact, use to happen the first time you saw a person of interest. Today, first sight may come after *first text* or first conversation on *twitter* or discovery on EHarmony.com. We live in such a different age than previously. This may not be all that bad. Looks can be deceiving, and what you see externally may be entirely different than what value may be discovered internally in a person. Of course physical attractiveness is not to be completely discounted. Remember this caution. Texting does not give away how annoying the person's voice may sound to you, and old photos can be posted on line. So go slow in making promises. Maybe talking on the phone before a first date is still a wise thing to do.

In the past, the second step was *first conversation,* and now it might be classed as *first in person* communication. Many of my older readers may be upset by the reverse of order, but it is not a real cause for alarm. It may boggle the mind of the older set, and be a mystery as why teenagers may be seated across the table from the person they are texting, but it is quite normal. Many younger adults can text faster than they can talk or think. They prefer to make initial contact by email or text, rather than in person or by phone. Rejection avoidance and self protection do make this a better option than the old traditional methods of: See girl; say hello to girl; hear girl giggle; then see girl ignore you, and run away. Texting eliminates some of that risk of public embarrassment. As one teenager said, "It is not near as embarrassing to be dumped on line as it is to be rejected publicly in front of your friends."

The next step in relationship development is *First date*. At one time that meant go some place, and spend money on your date. Surprisingly money as a scale of how much you like a person is not as necessary now. The trend among youth is to group date without pairing off in a secluded spot. I am impressed with teens that wisely protect themselves from temptation by hanging out together, and not pairing off so soon.

After the initial point of contact comes a *social* and *emotional connection*. If progress is to be made toward the wedding then a dating relationship will develop. The strongest bonding of two people will loosely follow a pattern of first socially spending time together. Observing each other in a variety of social settings makes a mutual discovery of common interests or obstacles. Do you find you have similar interests? Good, but if not this might be a clue to move along and look elsewhere. Emotional bonding occurs as you begin to notice you wish to share feelings with that special someone. Do you find yourself trying to tell that person what has made you sad, glad, or mad? Is that one of the first people you call or text, after something has stirred you emotionally? You realize you want them to see the movies which stirred your heart.

Physical touch and *romantic expressions* in our culture develop, and overlap as a relationship with the opposite sex merge two people toward a future fulfillment, and release of internal drives. If this happens earlier than this stage of a relationship they may cause you to be blind to some basic necessities for harmony in the days ahead. Even two cats can spend a night together but they often part ways in the morning.

Commitment issues of reluctance may reveal themselves as two people may be at different levels as *exclusive dating* (only dating the one person alone) and *pre-commitment* (called engagement) arrive. Sometimes, this stage is reached first by only one part of the couple. The discussion and observation of: "Where we are? Where are we going? How soon?" should be both open and honest. Unrealistic dreams are not real, and promises not kept always create long term confusion and possible pain. It is better to hurt a little now, than to have a big hurt put on you later. Selfishness and fear may cause reluctance, but in the long run it is important to be fair to each other by being brutally truthful.

The fulfillment of God's plan is arrived at in *marriage* and the *sexual experiences of marriage*. This does not end the development of a healthy relationship, but it provides a graduation of sorts into a deeper level of intimacy. If you noticed, sex is intended by God to come after the relationship is protected in the bonds of a married couple. This is not only best for society but is also the best order for a couple.

The merging together is completed with expressions and exploration of sexual fulfillment. This is protected within a marriage contract. Notice if the sex part comes sooner in a relationship than marriage, then it will often short circuit the health of the couple, by tricking them into the belief that they are suited in all the other ways of relationship development. Like electricity, sex can short circuit the process, and confuse the current of dating development only to discover later that the couple had less in common than they thought. I find couples who began in the bed on a first date mistakenly think their passion is a good measure of future bliss. Sadly many people end up telling a counselor that they really do not share much in common for the long haul. Sex is such a powerful experience that it makes your brains fall out into your pants.

Read: James 4:7-8 and 1 Peter 5:7-9

Pray: *"Whatever you want to pray."*

Single, Satisfied, and Stable

Choosing to live a life of being single is not abnormal. There may be many people who try to force everybody to be married like they are. That may be because misery loves company. There is a situation that is far worse than living the single life, and that is spending your life with the wrong person. It has been said that the closest thing to heaven on earth is a good marriage, and a bad marriage is as close as you can get on Earth to the other place.

If you are experiencing challenging times in your life as a married individual it might be wisest for you not to read the rest of this article. We are called to make the best of what we have, and if you are in a difficult marriage, then work to make it better don't just throw in the towel. Do not bail out too soon in order to become single again. The single life has its issues as well.

There are many reasons to spend your life as a solitary unit. Sometimes it is by our own decision, and sometimes other people make that decision for us. God does call people to be single for their lifetime just like He can lead people to be married to a person He wants for us to share in life's experiences with others as partners. Chapters Six and Seven of First Corinthians describes several marital options, and accompanying temptations with each. Among the list is the single life.

The great missionary and apostle, Paul, appears to be single by choice. It was permissible for him to marry but he chose not to be (1 Corinthians 7:7). This did not make him less of a person. Instead it allowed him more time to accomplish what the Lord wanted for him to accomplish. One of the best marriage counselor's I know was the pastor who married my wife and me. He has been single all his life of eighty three years.

If you are single do not let anybody tell you that you should get married because *two can live as cheap as one.* That statement is true only if one does not eat, and the other goes around naked.

Two problems which single people face are *loneliness* and *aloneness*. Aloneness involves the circumstances of being by yourself too much of the time. Be aware that many married couples face this as well. This is particularly true in military families, evangelists, researchers, sales people, and some other professions. Each group must develop a support network of friends, family, or others with a similar situation. Being single can be a blessing which allows you to have more time and choices, which you decide are important to you personally. Take initiative and control by eating in public places, and going out of your comfort zone in order to be around people.

Loneliness is more an emotional issue which is an internal feeling. Remember it is possible to be lonely in a room full of people. Sociologists state that in some situations the larger the population of a city, then the greater the sense of isolation. This is sometimes due to fear. During times of loneliness it is a time to take control of your self and circumstances. Reach out to others and allow them to meet your needs. Married people get lonely as well. I trust you realize that statement means you can meet your loneliness needs through friendship with someone of your own gender, and *not by hitting on somebody else's spouse.*

You might feel self conscious it this area. Some insecure spouses may even see you as a threat. This is so unfair, and ignores that many married couples cheat on their spouses with other married people as well. Singles plug your self into healthy married couples. Do not think you are a fifth wheel if you are the only single person in your group. Adults should act like adults, and be mature enough to not always be pairing up. Married couples should be sensitive enough to their single friends to include them in activities.

If you are single or single again stay sweet and not bitter. Advertising misery and guilt trips will not appeal to others and motivate them to include you in activities.

Read: 1 Corinthians 6 and 7

Pray: *"Lord, your word says that you supply every good thing I need, and I believe you always know best, so I pray that you would provide a mate for me if I need one, and keep me satisfied, and single the way I am if that is best."*

Checklists before you say I do

Despite the unknown that always becomes known sometime into the marriage, the following are a few ideas which might be helpful to discover in order to build a healthy marriage for your future. I am not sure whether these are best asked during dating or during the time of engagement; when final decisions about whether to go ahead into marriage or not are made. I call engagement a pre-commitment time to check the non-negotiable areas you might have about whether to marry or not.

There are a lot of items on most lists as desires we want in our future marriage partner, but they get crossed off the list easily if they are only preferences and not requirements. I have heard it said, "I will never marry a blond" until the right blond comes along, and that is crossed off the list as being just too narrow-minded.

I would not advise these on the first date but at some point try some on for style. Discuss moral convictions, religious beliefs, political views, moods, attitudes, values, hobbies, goals, restrictions, and levels of trust. Jealousy is a declaration of mistrust. If any of these areas seem totally out of your comfort zone, then you might want to move along toward another individual as a life partner.

People are becoming now what they will be in the future and the disagreeable roots may run so deep that they can never be removed. If you discover a chasm too deep to cross, then stop where you are. Do not pass go. Do not collect a marriage license. Issues we choose to tolerate in the short term may be hidden unexploded land mines in the long term.

Share information and views about your parents or early childhood circumstances, sleeping habits, debt, fears, decision making processes, hidden tattoos (especially if they have somebody else's name on your body), and your standards of collecting, or throwing away old items. At an advanced stage be open enough to examine each others calendars, check books, and your views of sex.

Remember life is a long term learning experience, not a quick laboratory experiment. After marriage you will never again say this is mine, but rather this is ours. Decisions are no longer made by asking what is best for *me,* but rather what will work best for our *we.*

Can both of you declare these four statements? I want to be me, and I want you to be you. I am not supposed to be you, and you are not supposed to be me. It is OK for you to be you, and for you to be different than me. I want to be the best me possible, and I want you to be the best you possible.

This is not meant to be exhaustive research or an interrogation, but a team exploration and self examination. It is more important that you become what you should be, and give yourself to some one rather than finding the right person to make you feel good about yourself. It is not finding the right person, but being the right person which makes for a success in marriage.

Read: James 1:5-8

Pray: *"May we trust each other enough to allow both of us to explore who we are, and to understand what makes us the way we are."*

Saying I did, before you say I do

There is a termite that attacks the future success of many marriages, which works underneath the surface, and eventually destroys many marriages. It is not really new, but it has become more prevalent, and is openly justified as being normal or even wise in today's World. It is called, "living together before the marriage ceremony". The sexual revolution of the 1960's led to this open type of low commitment relationship. While boomer parents may have experimented in this direction, they are often horrified by their children who see it as the norm. It has increased due to the lowering of moral and biblical standards. The theme for many is, "I want it all, and I want it now!"

There are usually three main justifications for this arrangement. Even some senior adults buy into this arrangement for economic reasons. Afraid they will lose social security benefits, or it is just cheaper than keeping up two apartments, or still not wanting to complicate the future of relations with their children, they decide to cohabitate. These economic reasons sound logical, but still compromise the integrity of marriage.

A security of sorts is the second reason for living together. You will always be sure to know who you will go out with on the weekend. It avoids some of the immediate drama of dating, and exchanges it for possible full blown dramas at a future time. This provides a sense of security for a couple until one person wishes to go on to a more permanent arrangement. If the other party is not as committed, then there are sometimes harsh and painful break ups.

The most common reason to live together before saying, "I do" is to prevent the tragedy of divorce. Often one or both of the live-in couple has witnessed how hard divorce can be by seeing the split up of their parents. This may be the most sincere, and logical reason for utilization of a one house with two unmarried people living together as if they were already married. When and if the marriage does take place the honeymoon is sure not quite as thrilling.

The major problem with this last rationale is all surveys, and research indicates couples who live together before marriage are twice as likely to end up in a divorce court, than couples who wait until married before living together. The very problem they seek to avoid is doubled. Wanting to help these couples I have tried to make a general conclusion. Because much success in marriage is based upon mutual trust, then their trial marriages began on the wrong basis. Not just a moral inconsistency, but also an intellectual miscalculation. It says to each other, "I do not know if I can trust you to be the right person for me, so you must be tested before we marry". Any future marriage is then begun with a suspicious foundation. In the long term it may be best to move out, until you are ready to move in for keeps.

Most couples who have been married very long admit they were on their best behavior before the wedding, and have since let it all hang out after they got married, because you can only pretend for so long. Many live-in couples still discover many surprises about each other after marriage.

If your marriage began on a false start, then do not be distraught. Realize you must go back, and work on developing a proper relationship of trust despite how it all began. Following God's order of marriage first, then experiencing life together utilizes His wisdom rather than our own. Be sure you are willing to share throughout all of life, then get married, live together, and work the rest of your lives meeting each other's needs.

Nobody can undue the past. God chose not to ever change the past, but He can, and does teach us from our mistakes, and takes all our past events, and works it together for our good, and His glory (Romans 8:28).

Read: Romans 8:28 and Philippians 3:7-14

Pray: *"Take us as we are Lord. Allow us to restart the process, and help us get to the place you believe we should be."*

That was then, and this is now

There are times and events in the soul of most marriages when you must put the past behind you, and develop a new starting line in order to begin again as if nothing happened before that point. There really is no complete way to put an egg back in its shell after it has been broken, nor is there any good way to place some events, and heartaches behind you except to smile, and just start again or reboot the system. The classic example in the Scripture is the book of Hosea. It pictures the untiring love God had, and has for His people through a radical picture of the love a husband had for his very wayward wife (especially chapters Two and Three).

This is not easy to accomplish, but I am convinced it can happen. It requires a huge amount of effort from both parties. If a marriage vow of forsaking all others has been broken it is a process of recovery which takes much time to restore. The offending adulterer knows when the sin affair began, and when it was definitely and definitively over. The wounded party can only guess if what they are being told is true. Even this guess is based upon uncertainty. It is not uncommon for the offending party to act defensive when they know they are being honestly repentant, and have cut off the improper relationships. They need to realize that the whole affair was out of the other's control, and because the facts came to them later; then working through the process of your spouse's forgiveness, and reestablished trust will take longer for them than it does for you.

"An offended brother is more unyielding than a fortified city" (Proverbs 18:19). The application of this verse applies here. If it took you six months to establish trust enough from your mate to get them to say yes to your proposal for marriage; then expect that it might take twice that amount of time for them to trust you again after you have thrown that trust under the bus of your own lust and selfish desires. You do not deserve a second chance. What you need is grace and forgiveness. These are not rights which you can demand. Take the crime as serious as you would take it, if the shoe was on the other foot.

Times come in marriages which may not involve a third person, but are none the less severe. Deep hurt and loss because of our actions and words may not be able to be placed back into the hourglass of time in a positive manner. Some experiences were done, and can not be undone. Perhaps both partners were guilty, and no amount of work will change what happened. It is possible however to look at each other with the hope that sometime that chapter will fade into the past as only a distant memory. Falling into each other's arms, and declaring a total cease fire, and the start of a new era causes a day of new beginnings to dawn.

This title opens up another area which faces many couples at the point they want to make a serious commitment to each other. Should I tell my future spouse about my previous sins, and sexually experiences? Unless you marry your first sweetheart without ever dating anyone else or ever facing the trauma of unwanted previous sexual experiences, then you must make the decision as to how much of your previous life should be shared with the one who will share your inner most life, and your total sexual history. It would not be fair to lie to a future sex partner if that unknown information will affect them physically. Serious information unrevealed only to come out later will drive a wedge in the area of trust.

The decision to silently put all past experiences behind you, and place a barrier between the past and the future, may be wise if this is agreed upon by both individuals. Let sleeping dogs lie is an old saying which works if you are never around those dogs that sleep or that you slept with. There may be wisdom in confiding in a trusted third party accountability partner about these events. That way each person knows their future mate has at least confessed all past known sin to somebody.

It may still be too painful to mention, or even psychologically suppressed if you suffered from sexual child molestation. Statistics say one in four women, and one in five men where sexually abused as children. Perhaps talking with a counselor to be sure the scars no longer haunt you would be appropriate. If you're past involved these problems, then remember you were the victim, and not the perpetrator. That was then, and this is now. Never allow the crime of another person to be paid for by the innocent one.

Read: Proverbs 18:19 and Hebrews 8:12

Pray: *"Savior, thank you that all our sins have been cast behind your back, and help us to never remember them or bring them up again."*

Breakfast bombshells

A dating couple should be aware that what happens in the early stages of a relationship is not always what may be expected in the future of their life together. My wife unfortunately learned that the hard way and perhaps too late. She now knows that I am not a morning person.

Within a few weeks after Judy and I married, we bought a trailer, so we could finish college in Bowling Green, Kentucky. It was the first major unwise financial decision, among many which we have made, but that is a topic for another day.

My wife began cooking at a very early age because both her parents worked. Being a great cook, and an early riser she got up the first morning in our new home, and prepared me a great big delicious breakfast. I smiled, and ate it all. The next morning was similar although it took me longer to eat it, because I kept pushing it around on my plate. By the third morning it was obvious to Judy that I did not like her cooking!

At that point I had to confess that I am just not a morning person. My best work has always been done after Nine o'clock at night. While my wife loves early mornings, and enjoys having coffee, and getting ready for the day, *I HATE MORNINGS*. Breakfast might be the most important meal of the day, but for me that means a piece of fruit, a cookie, or perhaps on a big day a bowl of cereal before I run out the door. I really do enjoy the typical big breakfast, if it is after noon.

I get that naturally from my Mother, and my Father who always worked swing shift at Ford Motors. Back when the rates went down after 11:00 at night we could always answer the telephone when it rang at 11:00, and say, "Hello Mom". Back when I spent one night every week at Mom's during seminary I would go to class; next I would study in the library until it closed at eleven, and then drive to the old home place on the South side of Louisville. Mom would be waiting ready for me to take her grocery shopping at the all night store.

Just remember what you see on a date after hours of preparation is not what you will spot the first thing every morning after marriage has begun. Before the shaving, hair combing, and time to put on make up there lies the true person you have pledged to spend you life with until death do you part. My advice is to get use to accepting each other for what you really are, and not what you can become after hours of work. Be willing to love what our mates are in their natural state, and not what we can become after intensive labor.

Read: Lamentations 3:19-27

Pray: *"Grant to my spouse the mercy to forgive me when I fail them, and grant to me the grace to receive what they offer to me, while allowing us both to have the wisdom to appreciate our differences."*

Absence makes the heart grow fonder

You have heard it said that absence makes the heart grow founder, but it also makes the mind stray away at other times. With our increasing mobile society there is a growing tread to be away from our spouse, who is designated to be our sexually fulfillment companion. This is not a brand new phenomenon. Times of absences from the home, and its marital benefits can be seen through out the Scriptures. (See Deuteronomy 24:5 and 2 Samuel 11:6-13).

God knew in the Garden of Eden that man would need a helpmate, and the sex drive within both male and female bodies is a very strong motivator. The temptations or urges which come when we are geographically distant from one another can heighten the pleasure of fulfillment when we are back in regular sleeping arrangements. Anticipation or longing for them can heighten the excitement for intercourse the next time the opportunity arises for sexual pleasure. There are some cautions in this area however.

Abstinence also creates a vacuum, and nature (human or otherwise) hates a vacuum. A vacuum cleaner will suck up dust, dirt, coins, or a stinky sock without regard to what you intended to accomplish. Men may have stronger sex drives, and less common sense than females, but both should be on the defensive to this temptation. It is much better to build a fence at the top of a precipice than a hospital at the bottom of a cliff. Regularly scheduled phone calls; traveling with credible work associates; staying out of places of temptation; leaving home with a kiss, and a good mood all help us keep proper perspective when absent from one another.

Times of abstinence may not be just for the reason of out-of-town business or having mileage between you. Paul mentions (1 Corinthians 7) that there are times for spiritual reasons when being deprived of each other's body may have a religious motivation. Times of illness, physical pain, stress, and even financial limitations can cause our desires to be placed in a holding pattern alone without normal marital relations. This is normally a temporary circumstance, and we are reminded in the chapter when it is required; it is so that we can *come back together* at a later time. This option should be by common consent, and never with a selfish motive, or as punishment to the mate. The Bible makes it pretty clear that if we marry, then meeting the other person's sexual needs should be our personal primary concern.

So sometimes abstinence is normal and healthy, but beware not to allow it to place the other person on the thin ice of temptation. When these times do arise remember *Suspicion oh suspicion* (sounds like an old Elvis song) should not be allowed to cause a problem when you do have the opportunity to reengage in sex. Seek to allow those times of separation to make the heart, and all of the anatomy to grow fonder.

Read: Deuteronomy 24:5; 2 Samuel 11:6-13 and 1 Corinthians 7:1-5

Pray: *"God, make me completely true to the vows I made on my wedding day to be faithful to my spouse, in order that we might celebrate without guilt the opportunities to restore the joys of the marriage bed when we return from being separated from each other."*

The Big 'D': When I do becomes I don't anymore

Divorce is like having major surgery without anesthesia. It heals, but is very painful, and may leave scars. Whether it is your first or fifteenth marriage, the same rules apply that dictate if you want a marriage to work; you must work on the marriage.

If you are the part of the couple which has not experienced a divorce in their home as a child or with a previous marriage, then you may not understand the deep hurt, and reservation which your partner may experience due to their experiences. It is unfair to threaten with the word, "Divorce" when it so emotional charged in your mate's mind. My wife has said that she does not believe in divorce; murder yes, but divorce no.

If you are the one who has the experience of a previously broken marriage then you may need to remember your new spouse is not the same as your previous mate no matter how much they may look alike; sound alike; say some of the same things; or remind you of a hurt from your history. They are *not* the same person. Do not make them pay for what happened to you before. These ghosts of the past may jump into your thoughts, but they may be placed there by the Devil to destroy yet another marriage.

There should be some learning which is accomplished from a previous marriage. That may be the only redemptive thing you bring from that previous marriage. *Stupidity* is doing the same thing again, and expecting different results. Remember, if you always do what you have always done, then you will always get what you already have gotten.

The death of a marriage, divorce, is similar to the death of the spouse. You should give your spouse a decent funeral, and it is normal to grieve. But it would be unhealthy to build a house next to the cemetery and live there. A divorced person is not damaged goods, and as in the death of a spouse, after a period of time, healing takes place so that you can go on with your life.

I expect if I die first my wife may move forward, and may date, and later marry again. I would hope that no body tries to ask her out while she is standing by my casket. It is probably a good rule of thumb to not date the same person more than twice in the first six months after a death or a divorce, and not to marry again for at least a year. This guideline helps avoid establishing a new marriage, before the grief from the first one is totally over.

There is a danger among some divorcees which pushes them to prove they are not rejects. This false assumption motivates a person to try and prove that somebody else wants them. Spite provides a poor start for a new relationship.

God never intended for a couple to say, "I promise you" get married, and then seven years and 2.4 kids later say ugly things in court about each other, and end up hating their once beloved. Yet it does happen. A man and a woman must begin together to make a marriage, but it can take just one person, and a lawyer to end it. It may rarely be totally the fault of just one person in the marriage which caused it to end in divorce, so it is best to try, and learn life style changes from the experience. Even if your responsibility for the failure was only 1% then you should take responsibility for that 1%, and learn from your mistakes. It may have fizzled before the finish because it had a fatal flaw from the first.

There are usually problems with expressing what we feel as a marriage dissolves. There may be times when we are very sad. We can be so sad, and disappointed that it leads to depression with all its side effects. Being mad at some point is normal as well. I have been told there may be times when you are glad it is finally out in the open or over at last. The difficulty comes when all these different emotions come on us at the same time. Just try to show me your sad, mad, glad face all at the same time. That is often what makes us think we are on an emotional roller coaster when going through a divorce.

Remember nobody every just gets a divorce. You get divorces even if you have only been married once. The formal legal divorce is granted when the gavel of the judge hits the table, and he says that the marriage is dissolved. The geographic divorce took place when you stopped living in the same house. The financial, sexual, emotional divorces may have taken place at all different times. If there are children involved, you will never be completely socially divorced. There will be times at hospitals, graduations, weddings, funerals, birthdays, etc. where you will be in the same social arenas as your previous spouse. For the sake of the children, and your own reputation act civil. Continuing unresolved conflict after the divorce or funeral is always wasted time.

Read: Exodus 34:6, 7; Malachi 2:15, 16 and Matthew 19:8, 9

Pray: *"God, I did not want this divorce any more than you did, but it happened, and I need you to help me begin to see I am still alive, even though my marriage is not."*

Four traps, pitfalls, and errors of Twenty year marriages

The only things which stay exactly the same year after year are probably already dead. We know that the only thing which stays the same; is that nothing stays the same. Perhaps it is a part of relational inertia. Things at rest tend to stay at rest, and things in motion tend to stay in motion.

The same is true in most marriages. It should come as no surprise that any marriage after twenty years will need a tune up, because things have changed. Continuously working on a marriage allows it to breathe, grow, and move forward. When you stop investing in a marriage it will only coast for a while, and then soon grind to a halt.

Taking a good inventory about your marriage every now and then, may be a good idea. It is possible to just go through the motions in a mechanical way, and your marriage partner may believe they are being taken for granted. One old boy told his wife when she complained about not hearing that he loved her said, "I told you I loved you when we got married, so if things change I'll tell you". We do like to be reminded vocally that things are still the same as they once were, and that we are still loved.

Remember ever time any major change takes place in the nature of the marriage it will necessitate redoing the controls, and relationships in the marriage. If you want to land safely then you can not keep a relationship in auto-pilot for very long.

The longer a marriage lasts, especially after twenty years there will be a stack of good memories piled up, but also bad memories which we regret, or cause hurt and anger in one, or both of the individuals. It is always by our own choice that we either look back in the direction of those good things, or toward those bad rerun episodes. They both are real, but what we allow to influence us; mentioning to each other or dwell on quietly in our minds will determine the worth we place on our marriage history. There is wisdom in not doing or saying things in the first place for which you will regret in the future.

Unrealistic expectations or non-acceptance of the diversity among each other is another problem that affects the long term marriage. If you have not noticed, now that you are approaching the 25th 'Silver' anniversary of your marriage vows; you're old now. At least you are older now, and much has changed sagged, begun to turn gray or fallen out. Major erosion influences take place. Body furniture is rearranged. So what, it happens to the best of us. Get over it and move on.

A fourth pitfall is the arrival of menopause for women, and midlife crisis for men. Both genders reach these challenges around this time in life, and do not have to cause great problems. Hormonal and emotional disruptions do create challenges, but should not derail a marriage of so many years of investment. Remember just how much your marriage has already withstood. If people would invest in what they have or can achieve, instead of bemoaning what they do not have, things would transition a lot smoother.

People who buy into the myth that it is the other person's entire fault, or they would be happier with this new love interest forget two important factors. If you would spend the same amount of work in sparking up the long time love as you are now putting in a new person, then you will no doubt get a better return on the secure investment of the past years. Also, you do know all the failures of your current spouse, but you have no idea what problems may be under the hood of a new flame which has only shown you their best features up to now.

Read: Joshua 24:15 and Proverbs 31:12

Pray: *"God, we have invested a lot of time into reaching the stage of marriage where we are now. Help us not to blow it at this stage of the game."*

Life goes on after the death of a spouse

This too is a part of Marriage. It may be a very sad part of any marriage, but inevitably many marriages will end by the death of the love of your life. An unnamed bride in Joel (1:8) dons grief clothes, and cries uncontrollably at the death of the beloved of her youth. It goes unsaid if this is the separation by death soon into the time shared in marriage, or after years of hills and valleys, and miles traveled together. It still casts a dark shadow of great sorrow. Please allow me to confess that I do not know this pain in my own life personally. My words come from what I have learned from listening to others who have told me their experience or through research. The closest I have come is the petrifying fear which has gripped me during those times my wife fell ill or had a near death experience. They have made us appreciate more what time we do have together.

No simple few lines can encapsulate all the possibilities in this area. The longer a couple are together the more memories are totaled up which makes the parting sweet from the vast memories we carry forward with us in the days and years of readjustments; and bitter because our lives have been so mingled together that it is hard to see a future without them with us to create even more special times. If your mate leaves soon into you time together, then the grief of wishes for a longer time to establish memories haunts us with empty dreams. Neither brief marriages, nor many years spent together can prepare us for parting with our lover because of their death. You are not in the minority as in time every marriage will come to an end. Remember although the grief is great, never having the love you shared is a disappointment greater than the loss you must feel now.

Rarely do both a husband and a wife die at the same time unless it is by the tragedy of an accident. Perhaps you may come to realize this is one final gift you could give to that person who was so precious to you. Instead of them suffering the lost of saying good bye to you, it was you, who out of no choice of your own, suffer the pain of being left behind in this world to carry on instead of them weeping over their loss of you.

Support groups and understanding the grief process through counseling may make us aware that whatever we feel is neither new nor unusual. Still, each surviving spouse must go through the valley of the shadow of death by themselves up to some point. Our faith strengthens us in the mysteries of life and eternity. For many the words of the Shepherd's Psalm (23), *"Even if I walk through the valley of the shadow of death I will fear no evil for you (the Lord our shepherd) are with me"*, remind us that He is there understanding our sadness.

How soon does the hurt go away? It leaves whenever it leaves. Each person takes as long as it takes them, and it is difficult for anyone else to tell you how long it will take. One thing I can be pretty sure about, and that is if your mate loved you, then they would not want you to build a house in the cemetery, but they would hope you could find the strength to move forward with you life, and live your future happily, until you meet again.

Lay aside the false guilt the Devil may try to use to punish you. Self-pity is counterproductive as well. Move forward, but do not make major changes too early while still in the valley of grief. Seek to forget the sights and sounds of the hospital, or the dying process, but remember always what good and positive things you shared together.

Whatever time you have been allowed to experience together in a healthy marriage; *it never seems long enough.* There may be words left unspoken or some times regrets that we wish were not part of our history, but in weighing it all together you can say, "Thank you God for the memories I still have which will grow sweeter ever day as I walk toward the future."

Read: Genesis 5, 23:1; Psalm 30:5 and Ezekiel 24:18

Pray: *"Lord, I am never by myself when I pray, because you have not left me even though I do feel all alone at times. Thank you for all the wonderful memories which I can still cherish. Help me now to go forward with my life as I carry on for the both of us, like they would want me to do."*

"Now go to work on your marriage and make it work!"

Dr. Jerry Adamson

About The Author

Dr. Adamson has served 46 years in Christian ministry in three states. He began Shepherd Staff Counseling eight years ago in order to assist physicians and pastors in their helping responsibilities with hurting people. In addition to speaking and counseling he currently serves as professor in his hometown of Louisville, Kentucky.

The principles in this work have been formulated in the trenches of real life counseling. After five degrees, thirty-eight years of pastoral experience, eight years counseling and teaching; plus ten years writing weekly newspaper columns; he became aware of the challenges and pitfalls of modern marriages. So, he determined his second book should assist couples in maximizing their marriages.

He and his wife, Judy, have three married adult children and five grandchildren. He is also the author of *Adamson Family Fables* and *Christmas Makes the Whole World Sing.*

CPSIA information can be obtained at www.ICGtesting.com
Printed in the USA
LVOW13s1306210813

348890LV00004B/13/P